Shells

An Illustrated Guide to a Timeless and Fascinating World

To the memory of Mariel

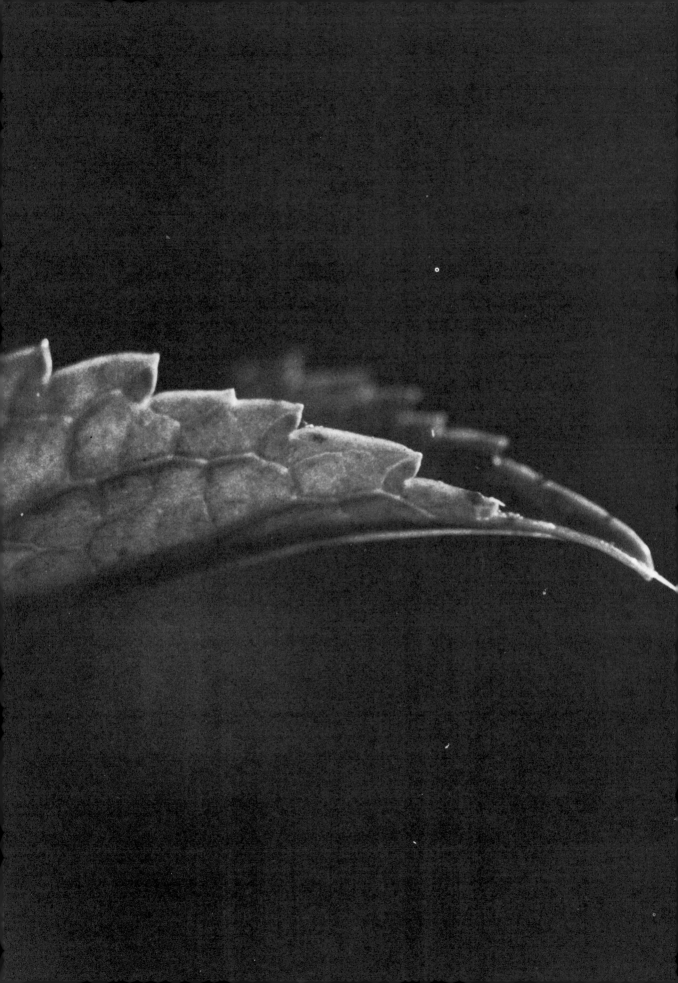

Shells

An Illustrated Guide to a Timeless
and Fascinating World

Mary Saul

Doubleday & Company, Inc.
Garden City, New York

Contents

Acknowledgements My especial thanks for invaluable encouragement, advice and helpful criticism are due to Dr R. Tucker Abbott who so kindly read the manuscript of this book; also to Mr S. Peter Dance, Mr T. E. Crowley, B.Sc., M.I.C.E., and Mr A. E. Ellis, M.A., F.L.S., who read it in part; and to the staff of the Worcestershire County Library Service for their helpfulness in obtaining so many of the books and references needed in preparing it. M.S.

Published by
The Hamlyn Publishing Group Limited
London · New York · Sydney · Toronto
Astronaut House, Feltham, Middlesex, England
Copyright © The Hamlyn Publishing Group Limited 1974

ISBN 0 600 38048 3
ISBN 0-385-05168-9 Doubleday

Library of Congress Catalog Number 73-19292

Text set by London Filmsetters Limited
Colour Separation by Colour Workshop Limited, Hertford,
Printed in Great Britain by Butler and Tanner Limited, Frome and London

Foreword

In the natural sciences, conchology has long been known as the 'queen of the natural history studies' for several good reasons. Man has had a close association with attractive seashells and edible molluscs ever since he ventured afield from his neolithic caves. Delving into the intriguing history of shells in art, literature, religion and science is a blend of true biology and a nostalgic recounting of how our ancestors worshipped and used shells in a hundred ways important to their survival.

It may seem startling to moderns that African wives could once be bought for 50,000 cowrie shells; or that the first form of Chinese money was purposely shaped like seashells; and there is a reason why mythologists have Aphrodite, the goddess of love, arising from the sea on a scallop shell.

Today, psychiatrists use shells to awaken in their patients the primitive erotic interests in material objects and to capture the attention of depressed patients. Modern conservationists, attempting to delay the final day of ecological destruction, use fresh-water mussel shells from our rivers to monitor the amount of radiation escaping from atomic plants. The future of our oceanic fisheries depends upon the understanding and protection of the extensive sea beds of clams and whelks that nourish our vital fish supplies.

By good fortune, the search for knowledge in this major oceanographic study has been aided by legions of amateur shell collectors and true lovers of nature. The history of conchology is replete with examples of outstanding personalities who have, by their great enthusiasm and devotion, contributed new-found species and many new biological facts. Mary Saul, the author of this entrancing book, can truly be considered a reincarnation of the warm-hearted and indefatigable second Duchess of Portland (1714–1785), who sponsored conchology in England and titillated the court of King George III. Mary Saul not only joins the literary company of Agnes Catlow who produced the outstanding *Conchologist's Nomenclator* in 1845, and Mary Roberts who charmed the Victorian scene with her *Popular History of the Mollusca*, but must certainly be considered one of the major modern contributors of scientific shell specimens to such outstanding institutions as the British Museum of Natural History, the Smithsonian Institution, and the Delaware Museum of Natural History in America. For many years Mary Saul and her husband, a police official in North Borneo, collected and classified strange shells from the limestone caves of the East Indies and the coral reefs of the south-west Pacific. Not only have new species been named after her, but the pages of such leading scientific journals as *Indo-Pacific Mollusca* are filled with her locality records and discoveries.

It is now her turn in the history of conchology to produce an intriguing and full account of how shells have influenced man in his many activities. Mary Saul has entertainingly recounted this historical phase of shell collecting and we many devotees to conchology will always owe her a debt of appreciation.

R. Tucker Abbott (du Pont Chair of Malacology)
Delaware Museum of Natural History, Greenville, Delaware, USA.

Introduction

The molluscs include such diversity of creatures as the pretty little periwinkle picked up among the rocks of the seashore; the common slug which eats up the sprouting greens in the vegetable garden; the great conch whose shell adorns the curio cabinet; the succulent oyster; the octopus writhing in his sea-cave; the humble garden snail; the cuttlefish, the squid and the delicate sea-butterfly, the pteropod. Together they form a great phylum of living creatures second in number of species only to that of the Arthropoda, to which all insects belong.

Molluscs began to evolve on our planet some 600 million years ago. During those aeons of time their descendants have learned to survive the vicissitudes of existence in water, salt and fresh, through every phase of heat and cold on land, through tropical rain and desert drought. They are a triumphant clan. They flourish today in a range of habitats wider than that of most other phyla. Their numbers appear to be as great as ever they were during the long ages when molluscs dominated the seas of the world before life on land had begun.

The story of their association with man begins with the prehistory of the human race, when the first human ancestors picked up pretty shells on some ancient beach and around the same time discovered that, within the living shell, there was a soft creature very good to eat. The empty shells, formed of a strong, durable, hard material, often smooth and sharp-edged or spiral and pointed, suggested a variety of practical uses. They were often extremely beautiful. Some were lined with a lustrous substance which repeated all the colours seen in he rainbow. Others were smooth and glossy or rough and spiked, glowing with bright colours and strange markings. They were good to look at, their shapes comfortable to the hand. They aroused the instinct to covet, to possess, to adorn.

There might be a lump of hard substance inside the soft flesh, sometimes roughly shaped, occasionally round and glowing like the full moon. The first humans to find the oyster must also have known the pearl, but it would slip from their greasy fingers and be lost in the midden heap of empty shells. Only when man had discovered how to pierce it and capture it on a thread could it become one of his most treasured possessions.

Some shells came to be regarded as magical objects, protective charms and talismans of fertility. In later societies they took part in religious ritual, became the insignia of power and appeared in the regalia of kings. Through the ages, their shapes and colours have inspired the painter and sculptor, the architect and the poet. Being regarded as precious and desirable they came to be used as money, one of them providing the longest-lasting and most widely used currency that man has ever developed. In addition to all this, the mollusc has provided man with a cornucopia of delicate and nourishing food rich in proteins.

Shells, or pieces of shells, are among the objects with which man has continuously adorned himself from the Stone Age days of prehistory right through the centuries to the present day. Modern man may no longer wear shells in his pierced earlobes, through his nose, round his neck or arm for both ornament and protection from evil; but he still wears shell in his tie-clip, his cuff-links and for the buttons of his shirt. His wife wears earrings, necklaces, brooches and bracelets made of shells, though she thinks of them not as fertility charms but as 'costume jewellery'.

Today, among the sophisticated societies of the modern world, shells have lost their ancient magic. Yet to twentieth-century man they have a magic of a different kind. To many people, the sight of a shell is evocative of happy memories of holidays on sunny shores, of the wide sea and the wave-swept beaches, of peace and relaxation under the sun, of the fresh sea-breeze and the tang of seaweed. Their lovely shapes and colours delight the eye and bring refreshment to the spirit, a respite from the stress and strain of daily life. They are symbolic of the murmuring sea in which all life began. Perhaps this is why so many of us like to have a shell or two around the house.

A book such as this can attempt only a brief outline of the fascinating story of the many and varied relationships between these marvellous creatures and the human race. Each of the following chapters merits a book of its own; most merit several. No two people would ever agree completely on the selections to be made from such a mass of information as exists on each and every aspect of the tale. So it is my hope to interest the reader sufficiently for him to wish to know more about some, or all, of these aspects. A short bibliography at the end of the book lists some of the works consulted in preparing this volume and each of these will lead to others.

In the text, scientific terms have been kept to a minimum. Species named are given their common names if generally known, also their Latin names, but not those of the authors (which can be found in the relevant reference books). Some of the terms used need a brief explanation:

Phylum a major primary division of the animal or plant kingdoms, such as Mollusca, Arthropoda, comprising organisms supposedly descended from a common ancestor and therefore sharing certain basic features of body organization which mark them off from members of other phyla.

Mollusca a phylum comprising six classes of soft-bodied, unsegmented animals usually having a hard shell.

Ecology the study of the mutual relationship between organisms and their environment.

Latin names every mollusc has two Latin names. The first is that of the genus (group) to which it belongs and the second is the name of its particular species.

Clam a general term applied to many kinds of bivalve molluscs.

Conch a general term applied to most large univalve shells.

Shellfish a term applied not to fishes but to many kinds of sea creatures such as molluscs and crustaceans which have a hard external shell or case.

Conchology or Malacology? because the great phylum Mollusca includes creatures so very varied in appearance and habit, it was not appreciated until quite modern times that the shell-less ones such as the octopus and the slug and those with a rudimentary internal shell such as the cuttlefish, squid and sea hare, were indeed related to the shell-covered bivalves and snails and belonged to the same phylum. The very word 'mollusc' has been misleading because it means 'soft-bodied' and was originally used only in connection with the shell-less species.

When it became necessary to find a suitable name for the study of this fascinating and diverse phylum, French naturalists of the eighteenth and early nineteenth centuries introduced two words: *conchyliologie* and *malacologie,* about whose definition and usage a controversy continues unresolved. In essence, the two words appear to have precisely the same meaning but many naturalists have held that conchology (to give the word its English form) concerns itself only with the shell and malacology with the study of the animal. But how it is possible to study the one without reference to the other, since it is the soft animal which makes the shell, has never been explained. Another French scientist, G. P. Deshayes, very sensibly underlined the crux of the matter when he asked how it was possible to make two sciences out of two inseparable things. However, the usage of these terms has now become largely a matter of status, malacology being the sphere of the full-time professional (a breed unknown when the word was coined). For the purpose of this book, however, the term 'conchology' will be used in referring to the whole study of the mollusc. It is the older word of the two and far better known to the general reader.

It should also be mentioned that there is no single species or genus to which the word 'conch' applies exclusively. It is a term which has, in its time, been applied to almost every kind of shell, from a mussel to the triton shells used as trumpets. Currently, it can refer to virtually any large, spiral univalve and especially to the Strombidae.

Prices and values, except where otherwise stated, will be referred to in those of their times. Fluctuating currencies make it ever more difficult to work out modern equivalents and the results, even if accurate, can be very misleading. It is possible, for example, to state that a native of a certain island would willingly pay £10 (in today's money) for a particular type of shell necklace. But this interesting information would be incomplete unless we also know something of the economy of his island and appreciate that the £10 represented to him a year's income. For our purpose these references serve mainly to indicate 'a great deal of money' or 'very little money'. If Julius Caesar ever did pay 60 000 gold pieces for the pearl he presented to his mistress Servilia, we do not need to know the equivalent in today's currency to appreciate that he paid an enormous price. We also know that Publius Clodius made a foolish and extravagant gesture when he swallowed one worth 10 000!

Where illustrations of shells occur, their sizes have been given in the caption wherever possible. Unless otherwise stated, the sizes are the average for the species concerned.

But to go back to the main theme of our story, we must start with a short account of the mollusc during those millions of years before man appeared on the scene.

Man and Mollusc Meet

Shelled creatures were already highly specialized when they began to appear in the fossil record some 500 million years ago. The first mammals emerged more than 300 million years later, while the man-ape or ape man, immediate ancestors of *Homo sapiens*, put in his appearance only during the last one, or possibly two, of those millions. When man and mollusc met, therefore, the mollusc was already a very old hand, and a very successful one, at adapting and adjusting to the hazards of life on this planet. Man, arriving, during the last tick of geological time, so to speak, is only now in a comparatively early stage of his evolution. Compared with the mollusc he has a very long way to go and, metaphorically speaking, a lot to learn.

Molluscs were among the first living creatures to have hard shells or horny outer cases which could leave those clear and reliable traces of their former existence which we call fossils. These shells, left on the seabed as their animals died; falling in their billions over millions of years; silted over with sand and every other dead organism dropping out of the teeming life of the ocean; embedded in sedimentary rock as the seas receded and the land rose; these form the most abundant evidence in the fossil record.

The fossilized shells of some molluscs may lie hidden intact through millions of years, preserving their original gloss and colour. Most fossils

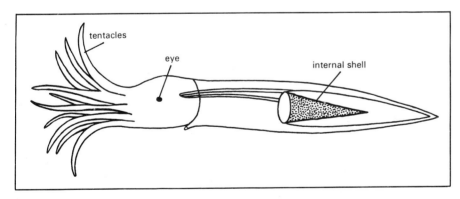

tentacles

eye

internal shell

that we dig from the rocks, however, are likely to be either colourless moulds or casts of the original tenant, the shell having disappeared long ago, dissolved away by water percolating through the rock. Sometimes just a faint shadow remains, a streak of whitish calcium in the rock. Sometimes the empty space is preserved intact, a perfect mould of the vanished shell. Sometimes the entire space fills up with other minerals which consolidate to form a cast of the original shape. Very careful dissection of fossil casts and removal of the outer layer can reveal the internal structure preserved in detail.

Left Reconstruction of a belemnite which existed approximately 200 million years ago.
Above Fossilized internal skeletons of belemnites, forerunners of the squid, found *in situ*.

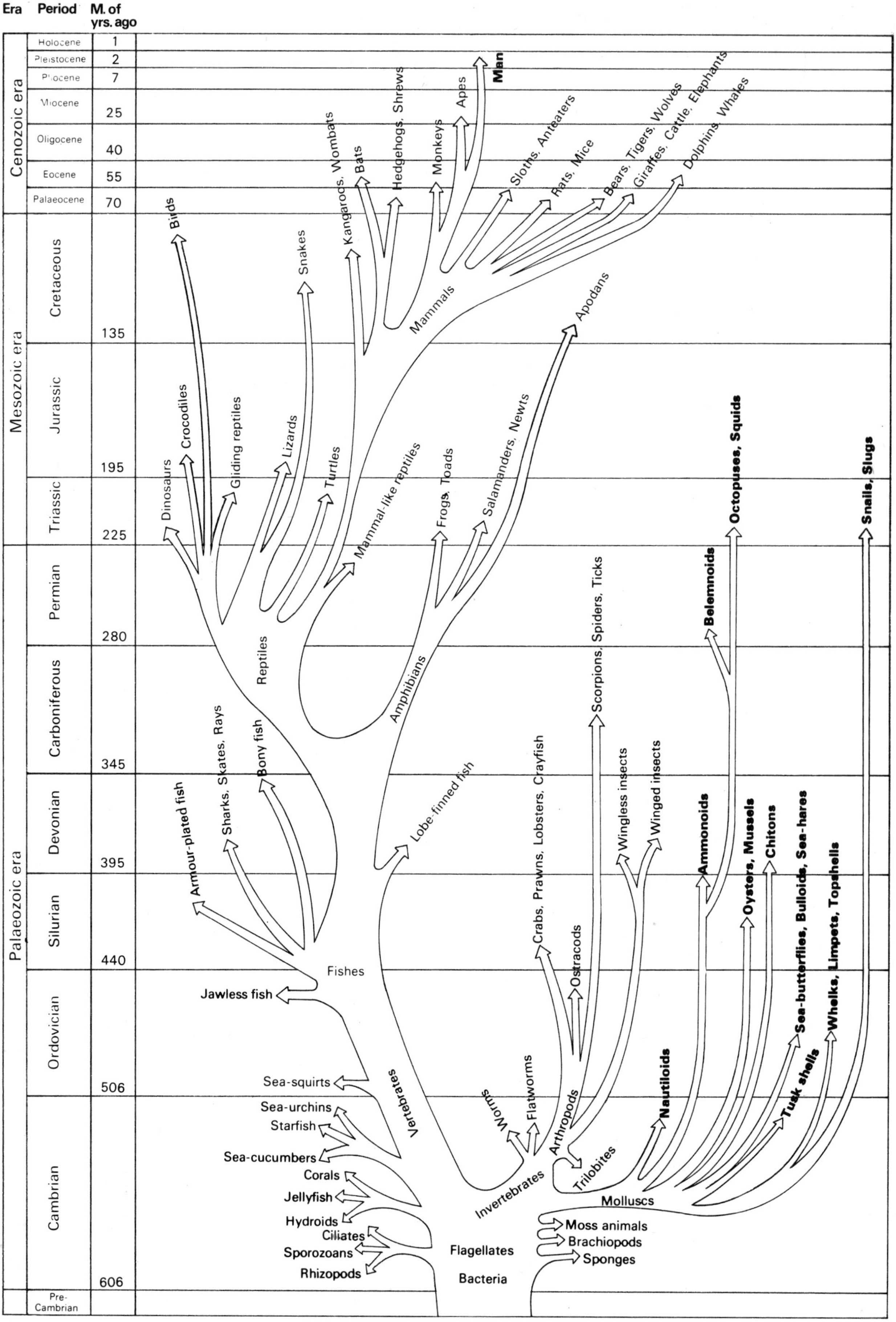

Era	Period	M. of yrs. ago
Cenozoic era	Holocene	1
	Pleistocene	2
	Pliocene	7
	Miocene	25
	Oligocene	40
	Eocene	55
	Palaeocene	70
Mesozoic era	Cretaceous	135
	Jurassic	195
	Triassic	225
Palaeozoic era	Permian	280
	Carboniferous	345
	Devonian	395
	Silurian	440
	Ordovician	506
	Cambrian	606
	Pre-Cambrian	

Man

Apes
Monkeys
Hedgehogs, Shrews
Bats
Kangaroos, Wombats
Sloths, Anteaters
Rats, Mice
Bears, Tigers, Wolves
Giraffes, Cattle, Elephants
Dolphins, Whales

Birds
Snakes
Mammals
Apodans

Crocodiles
Gliding reptiles
Lizards
Turtles
Mammal-like reptiles
Frogs, Toads
Salamanders, Newts

Dinosaurs
Reptiles
Amphibians
Scorpions, Spiders, Ticks

Octopuses, Squids
Belemnoids
Snails, Slugs

Armour-plated fish
Sharks, Skates, Rays
Bony fish
Lobe finned fish
Crabs, Prawns, Lobsters, Crayfish
Wingless insects
Winged insects
Ammonoids
Oysters, Mussels
Chitons
Sea-butterflies, Bulloids, Sea-hares
Whelks, Limpets, Topshells

Fishes
Jawless fish
Ostracods
Nautiloids
Tusk shells

Sea-squirts
Vertebrates
Worms
Flatworms
Arthropods

Sea-urchins
Starfish
Sea-cucumbers
Corals
Jellyfish
Hydroids
Ciliates
Sporozoans
Rhizopods

Invertebrates
Trilobites
Molluscs

Flagellates
Bacteria

Moss animals
Brachiopods
Sponges

From the fossil record, today's scientists can trace the evolution of the mollusc from its first known appearance early in the Cambrian period some 500 million years ago. These first fossils are formed from creatures already so highly developed at that time that, it is estimated, their evolution originated from ancestors which must have been developing at least 100 million years earlier. Among them are found the earliest forms of the Cephalopoda (squid, octopod, nautilus, etc.), the Gastropoda (snails) and the Pelecypoda or Bivalvia (bivalves), already a rich diversity of kindred creatures ranging from huge and heavy carnivorous nautiloids with shells up to fifteen feet in length (*Endoceras*), to small pelagic sea-snails.

The first of the nautiloids developed long, tapering shells like attenuated cones. They built their shells ever thicker and longer until, in Ordovician times, they reached the amazing length of over fifteen feet, the greatest length ever attained by a shelled mollusc. The interior of the shell was divided into as many as thirty-six chambers, each separated from the next by a wall or partition of shell known as the septum. Each wall was pierced by a small hole, the sides of which curved smoothly inwards to form a septal neck. The animal lived in the largest and last-made chamber, connected with the earlier and smaller ones only by a thin cord of flesh, the siphuncle, which passed through the holes in each of the septal walls from the first one built to the outermost one.

The inconvenience of dragging around this huge and unwieldy appendage was probably responsible for the evolutionary impetus which, over the next 100 million years transformed the long, straight shell through a variety of experimental curves into neat spirals like flat coils of rope. The gas-filled and buoyant chambers helped the animal to swim with ease and, aided by an ingenious method of water-jet propulsion, to move rapidly upwards or backwards.

Most of these shells were smooth on the outside or faintly ridged with the lines which marked periods of rest between spurts of new growth; the outer whorl of the spirally-coiled forms would take a final, majestic sweep almost covering the inner ones. Beneath so smooth and simple a curve the marvellous intricacy of the internal structure would scarcely be suspected.

Fifty to 100 million years later, in the Ordovician period, two other classes of the Mollusca had appeared; the Amphineura (chitons or coat-of-mail shells) and the Scaphopoda (tusk shells). It was during this period that the nautiloids reached their peak and began to decline. They developed both straight and coiled forms of extraordinary complexity and beauty. Today their class is reduced to the cuttlefish, the octopus, the squid and that wonder of nature the Pearly Nautilus (*Nautilus pompilius*); yet the fossil record includes over 10 000 species. Gastropods and bivalves continued to flourish and multiply in number of species as they have gone on doing right up to the present day. The Amphineura (chitons) are among the most primitive of the molluscs. They have left only about 100 fossil species and have never formed an important group. Neither have the Scaphopoda (tusk shells).

Later still, in the Devonian period, around 350 to 400 million years ago, new forms evolved from a nautiloid ancestor. These were the ammonoids, those exquisitely coiled and chambered fossils so greatly coveted by collectors, whose remains sometimes result in shell-opal once described as 'one of the most beautiful substances in nature'.

During the Mesozoic era, when on land the first small mammals began to appear, ammonoids flourished in the seas, developing a

Far left Evolutionary tree of the main animal groups. The thickness of the 'branches' do not denote numbers of animals within the groups.

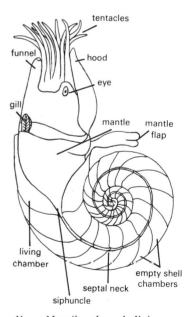

Above Nautilus, the only living externally-shelled cephalapod, partly extruded from shell, with the mantle partly cut away to show the gill and the shell in cross-section.

11

marvellous diversity of shape, sculpture and ornamentation, producing an explosion of rapidly evolving species and soon outstripping the more conservative nautiloids. They embellished the outsides of their shells with strong, angular ridges at the juncture of the whorls (suture line), with complex grooves and ribbings, with elaborately-fluted extensions decorated with sculptured knobs and nodules, with an infinity of delicate traceries and intersecting lines. In size the ammonoids varied from a diameter of a few inches to enormous cartwheels (*Pachydiscus*) six and a half feet across. These, with their huge nautiloid relatives, were the 'prehistoric monsters' of ancient oceans, the great carnivores of those

Above An almost perfectly preserved specimen of a fossil ammonite (8 inches diameter). *Right* A fossil ammonite (18 inches diameter) found *in situ* in Dorset.

warm shallow seas, rich with lime for shell building, which covered much of the world's surface 300 million years ago in the Carboniferous period. Under such conditions molluscs multiplied profusely. Towards the end of the Palaeozoic era gastropods and bivalves, including the first oysters, flourished in shallow waters; ammonoids, some crawling on the sea floor, others swimming near the surface, dominated the open seas. By the end of the Mesozoic era, some sixty million years ago, they had all become extinct, leaving the future to the more slowly evolving nautiloids and to the octopus and the squid which are the dominant cephalopods of modern times.

It was during the Mesozoic era too, that the belemnoids first appeared. These were the remote ancestors of the cuttlefish, molluscs whose shells had become modified to a thin cylinder with a pointed end like that of a well-sharpened pencil. This shell, called the 'guard', was secreted within the body of the animal as is the white internal shell or 'pen' of its descendant, the cuttlefish of today. The guards of some species vary in shape and many different genera have been identified. They are easily recognized in fossil beds and washed on to beaches among the pebbles; they are often taken for curiously shaped and banded pieces of stone. It is from the belemnoids that the gigantic squid of modern times most probably developed.

About the time that the ammonoids (exhausted, perhaps, by their tremendous evolutionary spurt) were declining to the point of extinction and producing strangely irregular and grotesque forms or uncoiling their shells, the first 'modern' molluscan forms began to evolve. Forty to sixty million years may still seem like an infinity of time almost beyond the imagination of man, yet, in the history of the mollusc, it is merely a chapter – a chapter covering only a tenth part of their life-story so far.

At the beginning of the Caenozoic era, oysters, cockles and mussels were established; the long, worm-shaped teredo appeared; so did the cowry, the murex, the volute, the spindle-shaped *Fusinus* and many other recognizable modern forms. Ammonoids had long since vanished from the seas, and the nautilus and the belemnite remained as the only common cephalopods. Horn shells (Potaminidae) and other species of the inter-tidal mud flats and the estuaries of rivers, continued to flourish. Fossils of the Miocene period, some twelve to twenty-five million years ago, have been found in great abundance. In some places they have formed 'shell banks' of fossils. About this time, the cone and fig shells also appeared.

A few of the forms which evolved during the past ten to twelve million years have become extinct, but the majority survive today.

To the scientists, the fossil record left in the rocks by untold generations of molluscs is invaluable. Mollusc forms of different periods were so abundant, so widespread throughout the seas of the ancient world, that their fossil remains can be used as an index for dating rocks.

Certain of these very widely distributed fossils, are so distinctive, developed and became extinct within such defined periods of geological time, that they are accepted by the geologist as markers by which rocks of similar age may be recognized throughout the world. By comparing and dating the fossil shells extracted from different layers in the borings from oil-well drilling with shells already found in areas known to contain oil-bearing shales or rocks, the great oil companies are able to direct their operations to areas promising success. So valuable is the shell record that such companies include palaentologists on their staffs of experts.

The abundance of ammonites during the Jurassic period, midway through the Mesozoic era, has led to the use of their fossil shells in identifying rocks formed during that period in different parts of the world. Fossil mussels which lived in fresh or brackish water around the swamp forests of Carboniferous times, later to become coal, have been of great use in tracing the area and direction of coalfields. The layers of mussel shells found in coal shales are referred to by miners as 'mussel bands'.

Usually, it is only the upper layers of rock which can be examined; the billions of fossils which must lie beneath are beyond our reach. But in certain parts of the world, tremendous upheavals, splits and cracks in the earth's crust, followed by millions of years of erosion, have brought to view layers of much older rock. The Grand Canyon of the Colorado river is perhaps the most famous example of this phenomenon. The Colorado runs through a gorge cut a mile deep through the crust of the earth, where the rock strata may be studied down to the earliest geological times.

The study of fossils is also part of the key to the study of the ancient geography of the world and its climate. Fossils of marine shells indicate the former presence of salt water; fossil corals that those seas were warm, for corals flourish best in sea temperatures around 75 to 80°F (24 to 27°C) and prefer the truly tropical waters where the temperature never falls below 68 F (20°C).

The reefs of fossil corals in Chicago for instance, are clear evidence that the sea once covered land now hundreds of miles from the nearest seashore and that, at the time, the climate was tropical not continental as it is now.

From the top of the Malvern Hills in the centre of Britain, between the mountains of Wales and the wide valley of the Severn river, one can see more of the surrounding countryside than from any other vantage point in the island. Four hundred million years ago, these hills, formed from ancient pre-Cambrian rock, some of the oldest in the world, were a string of islands surrounded by warm, tropical seas where corals grew and marine life abounded. Today, in the weathered limestone belts to the west, whole fields and slopes are covered with the fossils of brachiopods, trilobites, molluscs and corals. One can pick them up by the bucketful from every trench that is dug, from every field that is ploughed.

The biologist traces, from the earliest and simplest creatures, clearly evidenced in the fossil record, the story of their evolution into modern forms. Perhaps even more informative is the record of those which have disappeared forever, such as the ammonoids, those fabulous creatures which dominated the seas for millions of years without leaving a single descendant, yet whose physiology can be studied from the fossils which remain.

When earliest man encountered the mollusc, he was very far indeed from displaying any interest in its physiology. If, as is now suggested by some anthropologists, the African ape – ancestors of man, driven from their arboreal life by the terrible twelve-million-year drought which occurred during the Pleistocene period – had indeed been forced to adapt to a semi-aquatic life on the seashore, then the first near-human and human types would already have been well acquainted with marine molluscs as well as land snails.

The recent discovery in East Africa of a human-type skull over two million years old, puts back the emergence of human types at least twice as far as had previously been surmised; but whenever it was, their lives must have been indeed 'solitary, poor, nasty, brutish and short'. Almost the whole of their time and energy was devoted to the search for food. The need to find enough to eat was their chief preoccupation and a main cause of their wanderings. A brief pause to clean up the short-lived supplies of fruits or nuts in their seasons, to clear the camping area of anything edible, and they must be on the move again or starve.

As they grew more adept, they could learn how to catch and kill certain animals, but it was a chancy business. There was, however, a rich, reliable and lasting source of protein food available to them – that of the mollusc.

How fortunate were those early food-gatherers when they had the tremendous good luck to stumble upon rich beds of oysters, mussels or cockles. Endless supplies of the most delicate food in the world there for the taking! Nothing to do but break open the shells and suck out the succulent morsels. An occasional hunting trip, perhaps, or a visit to nearby woods or forests to collect fruits and roots for a change, but always with the happy thought that there was plenty of food back home.

People of Stone Age cultures all over the world left as evidence for their descendants the huge heaps of discarded shells which rose higher and higher with each succeeding generation. The sites of such prehistoric encampments can be found in the coastal areas of almost every part of the world, along the shorelines of ancient seas, edging the beds of long-vanished lakes where vast conglomerates of freshwater

mussels once flourished. Some are hundreds of yards in length and are estimated to have taken centuries to form. They are the debris of people who lived, quite literally, squatting on the tops of their own rubbish heaps.

In northern Europe they are called 'kitchen middens' and in them have been found, among the billions of broken shells, bone and stone implements and the oldest pottery vessels yet discovered. At Skarra Brae in the Orkney Islands, people made little huts roofed with the ribs of stranded whales, but the shell heaps of succeeding generations grew so large that eventually they engulfed the huts and the inhabitants formed tunnels through the shell mound through which they had to crawl to reach the entrances of their homes. Very early humans who occupied the huge limestone caves at Niah in Sarawak about 40 000 years ago, left, among their debris, the charred shells of snails which appear to have been roasted whole before eating. A shell mound at Newhaven in Sussex is formed mainly of limpet and other shells, together with the bones of animals. In Scotland, shell middens have been gradually carted away by farmers who found the crushed shells useful as manure and as a top dressing for their fields. On the other side of the world, shell mounds containing many tons of shells were noted by Darwin when he visited Tierra del Fuego and an early traveller in Australia described a hill of broken shells covering nearly half an acre and ten feet high in places. It was situated above a bed of cockles and on the top of the mound could be seen the fireplaces where shells had been cooked, with some of the last-collected heaps of shells beside them as though ready for the next meal.

Along the banks of the Kentucky and Tennessee rivers in America are mounds formed from the discarded shells of freshwater mussels which are thought to have originated some 7 000 years ago. These were specially favoured locations where the still-nomadic tribes could settle, during times long before the development of food growing made permanent or even seasonal settlements a practical possibility.

It was not only as food, however, that the mollusc was so highly esteemed by our primitive ancestors. Man, at every moment of his history, has had a feeling for beauty, shape and colour. He has always been attracted to the strange, the mysterious, the rare. He has, deep in his nature, the urge to possess objects which will add to his esteem in the eyes of his fellows and which others will covet. All but the most progressive and sceptical feel the need for protection against the unknown powers of evil. The shells of molluscs supplied all these needs. Picked up on beaches for their beauty, carried inland by wandering tribes, they became strange and rare when handed on to later generations who might never have seen the sea. In some of them, a mysterious, murmuring sound could be heard. They were treasured as supernatural objects along with such other strange phenomena as pieces of the meteorites which fell from the sky, colourful pebbles, lumps of rock crystal and obsidian from locations lost in the mists of tribal wanderings or passed from hand to hand in the very earliest beginnings of 'gift exchange' or trading. Such objects provide most valuable evidence to the ethnographer in his study of the wanderings of early humans and the spread of their kindred cultures throughout the world.

Shell objects found in a grave on Ranongo Island, Solomon Islands.

In France, during the building of a railway line in 1867, a Cro-Magnon grave, some 30 000 years old, was uncovered. In it were the skeletons of three men, a woman and a child, all of whom had been murdered. Their bodies had been given a ritual burial, sprinkled with red ochre and surrounded by weapons, tools, ornaments made from the teeth of animals and a necklace of shells. Another Cro-Magnon grave, also discovered in France in one of the most ancient cave-dwellings yet recorded, contained a helmet shell (*Cypraecassis rufa*) which is found only in the area of the Pacific and Indian Oceans and must have passed through many pairs of hands on its long journey from East to West.

The Tiger Cowry (*Cypraea tigris*) found in a prehistoric pit-dwelling in England, must also have been brought there from the Indo-Pacific, while cowries found in palaeolithic graves at La Madelaine and other sites could have been obtained no nearer to France than the Red Sea.

An Ice Age grave in Bavaria contained the skulls of thirty-three human beings, men, women and children, all of whom appeared to have died violently, perhaps in some ritual killing. The skulls had been placed with the faces turned to the west and around one of them lay a semicircle of small mussel shells which had been pierced as if they had been strung into a necklace.

Such shells, found among the treasured possessions which were buried with the dead, provide clear evidence that the peoples of those ancient times were very widely travelled, and that extensive routes existed along which such highly-coveted objects and the luxuries which were probably the very first articles of trade, could be passed.

Sometimes the demand was not simply for magical and exotic objects from far-away places, but for a specific kind of shell, the wearing of which had become widespread. Such was the Thorny Oyster (*Spondylus gaederopus*) which became so popular among the early Neolithic farmers of the Balkans, Macedonia, Bulgaria and the Danube basin. It is thought that this devotion to the *Spondylus* shell may have been passed down through tribal memory from ancestral groups who had lived along the shores of the Mediterranean. As these peoples spread north and west, they carried the cult of the *Spondylus* shell as far afield as the Rhine, the Oder and the middle Dniester in Russia. So great was the demand for them, that some form of barter trade must have developed with tribes living around the Mediterranean and beyond. With the peasant farmers of the Middle Neolithic, the *Spondylus* shell was as popular as ever. Supplies continued to find their way along

Above Two Pleistocene fossil gastropods found in the Red Crag, Suffolk. Right: *Neptunea antiqua* (dextral shell, $2\frac{1}{2}$ inches long. Left: *Neptunea contraria* (sinistral shell, $3\frac{1}{2}$ inches long).
Middle A Cretaceous fossil belemnite (*Actinocamax plenus*, $2\frac{1}{2}$ inches long) found in chalk in Kent.
Below A fossil ammonite, sectioned and polished to show its internal. chambered structure.

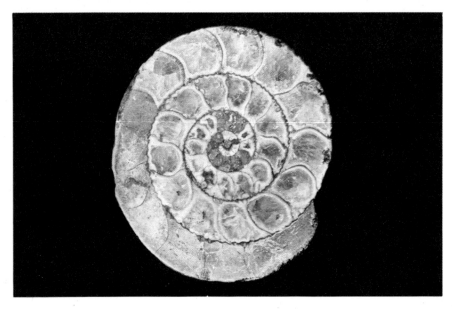

the old trade routes and as these cultures spread ever westward, they were eventually reaching settlements in Belgium, France and northern Italy. In Ligurian caves they have been found together with clay figurines of the earliest deity, the Mother Goddess.

In this context, it is interesting to note in an Aztec manuscript listing tribute paid by subject peoples, an item of 800 red sea-shells. The pictograph for the shells is a formalized drawing of what looks very much indeed like a Thorny Oyster.

The cult of the tusk shell (*Dentalium*) is of later origin and one of its earliest examples is the beautiful necklace found at Kirokitia in the Middle East, a very early urban settlement dated about 5 500 BC. This is a most artistic and elegant piece of work, the tusk shells being strung in groups of four or five, all tapering in the same direction and separated by clusters of carved cornelian beads. In a grave of about the same period at Mount Karmel, two of the skulls wore elaborate head-dresses of *Dentalium* shells. Headbands and necklaces have been found in similar burial places at Eynan and in a grave site at Mount Hernon an earlier interment had been pushed aside to make way for a new occupant wearing a handsome tusk shell head-dress.

Tusk shells are the only class of molluscs which are formed with a hole right through the centre, ready for threading; they need no grinding, breaking or piercing. Their slender, tapering shape, the ease with which they could be made into ornaments and the convenience of the hole, made a strong appeal to primitive peoples.

In America, the cult of the tusk shell, spreading from tribes living on the west coast around Seattle, developed into a special form of currency which will be discussed in chapter six.

That some shells were considered sacred as well as precious or ornamental is indicated by their association in so many graves and ancient temples with sacred images, figurines and other cult objects. In a neolithic deposit at Phaestos in Crete, sea-shells are found in juxtaposition with a clay image of the Great Goddess, libation bowls and a piece of meteoric iron such as was highly prized by primitive peoples because of its supposedly miraculous origin.

The second town to be built on the site called Jericho was inhabited between 6 000 and 4 500 BC by a race of small-boned, long-headed people with delicate features and sophisticated faces. This we can surmise, because among the remains of this settlement were found seven skulls which had been most artistically and skilfully restored with clay to a semblance of life. The modelling is exquisitely done and the eye sockets have been filled with shell 'eyes'. In one case, cowry shells have been used, the shells embedded so that the slit of the shell appears as a half-open eye. In others, pieces of shell have been shaped and inserted in such a way that a slit down the middle of the eye gives so vivid an impression of the pupil that it can almost be felt to be casting a slyish sort of glance.

All around the coasts of the Mediterranean from north-west Africa to Spain, southern France, the Rivieras, southern Italy and the islands of Sicily and Malta, an early and unique culture left its distinctive traces in the form of pottery decorated with impressions made by the wavy edge of the shell of one of the bivalves called heart shells (*Cardium*); but primitive man was to find another use for certain shells which would develop into a cult of worldwide importance.

Someone, somewhere, probably in the area of the eastern Mediterranean, made the remarkable discovery that blowing into a large, spiral univalve shell which had had its point broken off, produced a

A decorated conch shell, thirteen inches long, found at the Spiro Mound, Oklahoma, made between 1200 and 1600 AD.

18

splendid and awe-inspiring sound, the like of which had never been heard before. The shell trumpet had been sounded. Its voice would be heard in almost every part of the inhabited world; its use would continue from neolithic times up to the present day. Some made their trumpet simply by grinding or sawing off the tip of the pointed spire and blew straight down the shell; others bored a hole into one of the upper whorls near the tip and blew into the shell from the side. The same deep, booming sound resulted and could be heard over long distances. Such an object was to have a thousand uses, from the deeply religious to the simple and practical.

Crete is believed to have been the original home of the shell trumpet, but its sound was soon to be heard all over the Mediterranean and its use became widespread. The Mediterranean Triton Shell (*Tritonis variegata*) was chiefly used and is frequently found in association with human remains dating from Neolithic times. Two hundred broken shells and eighteen unbroken ones were found in one Italian cave alone. Each one had had its apex removed and had been clearly intended for use as a trumpet. The favourite shells for use as trumpets were in India, the Sacred Chank Shell (*Turbinella pyrum*); throughout the Indo-Pacific, the largest of the triton shells (*Charonia tritonis*); and in America, the Queen Conch (*Strombus gigas*). Other species of suitable form were also used and many were carried by migrating peoples to lands far distant from their home waters.

In New Guinea and Indonesia, where evidence of megalithic culture is to be found in some places along the coasts, the monuments have been sited only in places near to the oyster beds where pearls could be found. In Central America, Mexico and Peru, the purple shell-dye was used, the shell trumpet sounded and pearls were held in high esteem. In ancient Mexico, the people were especially skilled goldsmiths and dyers, using the purple dye of murex shells as did the Phoenicians of the eastern Mediterranean. The Gaelic king of ancient Ireland, who was said to have been the first to smelt gold there, is also reputed to have introduced the craft of making the purple dye which was still used in country districts until not much more than a century ago.

Similar cultures can be traced in Europe from Spain to the Caucasus; in the East from Manchuria and Japan to the Philippines and throughout the Pacific. These people settled where they could find copper and gold to work, where they could search for pearls and make dye. In these places they raised their huge stones to the sound of shell trumpets.

Thus the discoveries of the archaeologist and the ethnographer provide convincing evidence that these various special uses of shells were disseminated through the world, along with other customs and beliefs, by the builders of the megaliths and that their culture stemmed from a common ancestor.

Above Flat Periwinkles (*Littorina littoralis,* usually less than 1 inch long) which are commonly found in the middle and top regions of the lower shore.

Right Group of Flat Periwinkles (*Littorina littoralis*) showing the colour variation which can occur.

Far right Nudibranch sea slugs (0.8 inches long) from the coral reefs of Mozambique, Africa, feeding on hydroids. The cerata on their backs contain stinging cells, derived from their prey, which protect the slugs.

The Biology of Molluscs

A question long debated among biologists is that of the origin of the molluscs: from which branch of the tree of evolution did they develop? They do not appear to be related to the creatures of any other phylum. The study of their biology has fasincated the student of natural history from the time of Aristotle.

One theory has held them to be related to the segmented worms which duplicate every organ in each segment of the body. The recently discovered Monoplacophora, gastroverms as they have been named, may prove to be the missing link. Living descendants of a class believed to have become extinct 400 million years ago, they have segments similar to those of the annelids such as earthworms.

All molluscs were originally marine animals. Most species living today have evolved over the last few million years and are still very similar to fossil remains found in Pliocene rocks, some thirty million years old.

In the number of their species the molluscs are second only to the arthropods which include insects, spiders and crustaceans. It is difficult to estimate the number of species living today for modern research raises questions as to what, exactly, constitutes a species. Moreover, some variously named species are now shown to be synonymous and the relationships in many groups have yet to be determined.

Estimates of the experts range from 40 000 or 50 000 living species up to 100 000 or more. Taking an average of a probable 70 000 species, more than half are gastropods (snails, slugs), a third are bivalves (clams, oysters), and the remaining sixth includes the chitons, tusk shells, cephalopods (squid, octopus) and the tiny group of gastroverms mentioned above.

They have no standard shape or size, indeed no other phylum contains a more varied range of creatures. Though not very high in the evolutionary chain they have developed successful and often highly specialized ways of life adapted to a very wide range of habitats. All classes are found in the sea; gastropods and bivalves in fresh water as well; but only some of the gastropods have adapted to life on dry land.

Despite the differences in their appearance, the body plan of all molluscs is basically the same and differs from that of all other invertebrates. Their soft, unsegmented bodies would appear to be the only thing they have in common and it is these adaptable bodies rather than the hard shells covering most of them which have enabled molluscs to survive and thrive.

The body is formed of a combined 'head-foot' and the internal organs are covered by a shawl of flesh called the *mantle* which in most forms secretes a shell. This mantle is a unique characteristic of most molluscs, a feature which distinguishes them from other groups of living creatures. It has been described as covering the animal in much the same way that a roof with overhanging eaves covers a house. The space 'underneath the eaves' is called the mantle cavity. It houses the gills of marine and fresh water species and is modified into a kind of lung for terrestrial snails and slugs and some freshwater ones too.

Another feature characteristic of molluscs, though not of all of them, is the *radula*. This is a horny, ribbon-like structure inside the mouth which is chiefly used for rasping up fragments of food. It is set with tiny, sharp teeth, sometimes hundreds of rows of them and acts rather like a band moving over a pulley, with newly formed teeth continually moving forward to replace the front ones as they get worn away.

Some molluscs are strictly vegetarian, others are fierce carnivores and sometimes cannibals. Others are scavengers, feeding on dead fishes and crabs or on dead organisms drifting down through the water. Many, like the bivalves, obtain their nourishment by filtering particles of food from the water which they continually siphon in and out. The shipworm (*Teredo*), however, confined to its narrow tunnel, eats the only thing it has plenty of – wood.

Most molluscs secrete a shell which protects the soft animal within. Many other groups of creatures have also developed hard outer coverings or external skeletons to support and protect. Most of these enclose the animal completely and restrict its activities and its growth. It is the molluscs which have overcome this disadvantage by evolving shells which have an aperture through which both head and foot can be extruded and which can be continually enlarged to keep pace with the growth of the body. The head and foot, emerging for feeding and moving, can be quickly withdrawn at need.

It is mainly in the mantle and especially at its edges, that the complex cells which secrete the material of the shell, are located. The shell of a mollusc is formed almost entirely of calcium carbonate exuded as a semi-liquid substance which hardens very rapidly as soon as it is exposed to air or water. It is formed simultaneously in three layers. The outer layer is a horny skin of conchiolin, dull brown in colour and partially or completely obscuring the colours and markings beneath. This outer layer, the *periostracum*, acts as a protection against the carbonic acid in water which would dissolve or damage the main structure of the shell. In nature the beauty of many shells remains hidden until the animal has died, the action of sea and sand has worn away the periostracum and the waves have cast the dead shell upon a beach.

Not all shelled molluscs form this horny layer. The cowries, for example, and other groups of molluscs which have shining, glossy shells, keep their mantles spread protectively over the outside.

The central layer, formed of crystals of calcite or aragonite, is called the *prismatic* layer and is most often white and opaque. The outer surface of it, lying next to the periostracum, may be rough, ridged or decorated with knobs and spines; or it may present a smooth surface embellished with patterns, colours and intricate designs.

The innermost layer, lying next to the mantle of the animal, is the *nacreous* layer, formed of many thin coats of crystals. It is this layer, formed from cells over the whole of the mantle area, which constitutes in many shells the exquisite pearly nacre known as mother-of-pearl. If not pearly, this layer is always fine and smooth and the mollusc continues to add to it as long as it lives.

The growth of the spiral shell begins at the nucleus, tip of the spire, and continues by adding to the aperture and widening it as growth

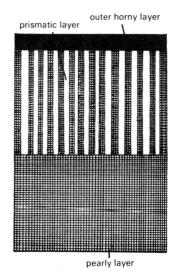

The layers of the molluscan shell, secreted by the mantle epithelium.

Right Final stages in the growth of the spider conch (*Lambis chiragra*) are shown from top right in an anticlockwise direction. When the body of the shell is complete, the mollusc builds out finger-like extensions from the outer edge of the aperture, which are at first frail and hollow but are gradually filled until solid.
Below Tusk shells (*Dentalium elephantinum*, 3 inches long).

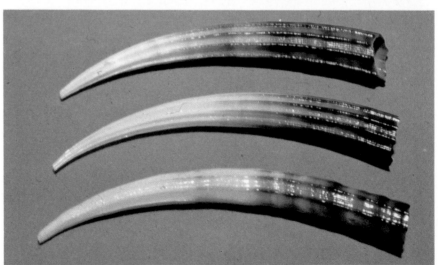

Left The Whirlpool Ram's-horn Snail (*Planorbis vortex*) showing the body coiling around shell spirals.
Below A sea hare (*Aplysia punctatus* 6 inches long) which ejects a purple slime when disturbed.

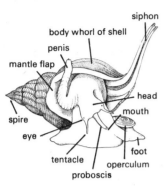

Diagram labels: siphon, body whorl of shell, penis, mantle flap, spire, eye, tentacle, proboscis, operculum, foot, mouth, head

Above European Whelk (*Buccinum undatum*, shell 4 inches long) in the crawling position with extended proboscis. The penis is usually tucked inside the shell, but is outside here to show the structure.

proceeds in an ever broadening spiral. Should the shell become damaged during growth or by some accident, the mollusc can often make an effective repair, filling in and strengthening cracks with extra layers of shell, patching broken edges and reinforcing the small holes made by marine worms or other predators.

Living molluscs are divided into six classes of which Gastropoda is by far the largest and the most widespread. It includes all snails and slugs, whether living in salt, brackish or fresh water, or on land. Most have a one-piece shell, spirally formed; some a rudimentary plate of shell hidden within the flesh; while others have ceased to make a shell at all. They range in size from organisms no bigger than the head of a pin to large creatures such as the False Trumpet (*Syrinx aruanus*) of Australia which grows to over two feet in length and is the largest of the shelled gastropods.

The animal has a head with two tentacles or feelers with a light-sensitive 'eye' at the base or at the tip of each. Below and between the tentacles is a muscular tube, the *proboscis,* which can be extended for feeding and has a mouth at its tip. The front part of the mantle extends to form a tube, the *siphon,* through which a continuous supply of water is drawn into the mantle cavity and to the gills which lie there. In land snails and slugs, which have two pairs of tentacles, the modified mantle cavity acts as a lung.

The gastropods which grow a spirally coiled shell have undergone a very curious form of distortion during the early stages of growth. Known as *torsion,* this has resulted in the whole of the internal organs, the visceral mass, being rotated through an angle of 180° while the head and foot have stayed in their original positions. Thus the soft visceral parts are pushed up into a hump and the anus comes to lie above the mouth instead of at the opposite end of the animal. The organs on one side of the body fail to develop and the spirally coiled, asymmetrical shell has evolved to enclose and support this strangely twisted body.

Both snails and slugs move around by the gliding motion of a large, fleshy *foot,* well supplied with the mucus which can be seen forming silvery trails wherever they have passed. Some of the shelled species form a disc of horny or porcellaneous material like that of the shell itself,

A Common Limpet (*Patella vulgata*, 2 inches long) clinging to a rock with a scar left by another limpet.

attached to the upper part of the foot, at the rear. This is the *operculum*, a neatly-fitting 'trapdoor' which in some species exactly closes the aperture of the shell when the animal withdraws inside.

The shell-less gastropods and those with but a rudiment of shell include not only the land slugs best known for their activities in the vegetable patch, but a variety of marine forms many of which are remarkable for the brilliance of their colourings and the beauty of their patterns. Some have mantle edges which extend wing-like on either side so that they appear to flutter gracefully through the water like colourful butterflies. Their gill organs take the form of feathery fans, ferns, plant and flower shapes of infinite delicacy which vibrate with every movement of the water. There are also the sea-hares (*Aplysia*) which browse among the seaweeds and so match them in colour and movement that they seem to disappear into them.

The second largest class is that of the Pelecypoda, the bivalves which live only in water, from salt to fresh. These are characterized by having two shells or valves which cover the right and left sides of the animal and are hinged together at the back by an elastic ligament of horny substance. One species, the Giant Clam (*Tridacna gigas*), is the largest of the shelled molluscs and may reach over four feet in length.

The two valves of shell grow simultaneously, each radiating outward from the *umbo*, the point at which growth began, beside the hinge.

Far left Sea slug
(*Hexabranchus adamsi* 4 inches
long) from Mozambique,
Africa. This species is able to
swim well by undulating its
body.
Left A bubble-shelled snail
(*Bullina ziczac* 1.7 inches long)
found near Mauritius, Indian
Ocean.
Below Close-up of the Giant
Clam (*Tridacna gigas*).

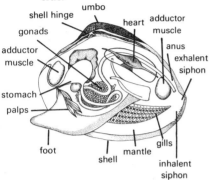

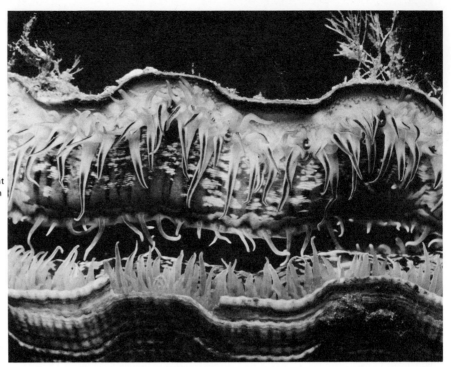

Inside, near the hinge, many bivalves have 'teeth' which help the two valves lock firmly together. These take many forms, from a simple 'ball and socket' device to elaborate interlocking formations.

The shell does not always grow at the same rate. Usually growth slows down during colder seasons when the mollusc does little more than add a thickening to the outer edge of each valve. When shell-making speeds up again with the advent of warmer weather, the thickened edge shows up as a distinct ridge or 'growth ring'. Such a ring may be formed at any time when normal growth has been disturbed.

It is the elasticity of the hinge ligament which springs the valves apart but it is two muscles inside, one attached to each valve, which draw them tightly together when the animal closes its shell. These *adductor* muscles are of extraordinary strength relative to the size of the mollusc and have given rise to many sayings about the tightness of the clam and the closeness of an oyster.

Most bivalves do not move around very much. Some of them cement themselves to rocks; others spin fine, tough threads, the *byssus*, with which they anchor themselves firmly to stones and corals or deep into the sand and rubble of the seabed. Some spend their lives buried in sand or mud. Consequently they obtain all their nourishment from the water and have no need for head, mouth or *radula* teeth·like the gastropods. The muscular foot is used not for gliding but for digging into sand or mud for maintaining position or as an anchor against the pull of the surf. Sometimes it is used to move the bivalve short distances, either by digging and hauling or as a paddle, pushing the mollusc in short hops over moist sand.

The remaining four classes of molluscs have far fewer representatives.

Amphineura, the chitons or coat-of-mail shells, sometimes known as the armadillos of the sea, are distinguished from all the other classes by the row of eight overlapping plates of shell arranged along their backs. They are the least complex of molluscs. The oval-shaped body is bilaterally symmetrical, having both sides alike with the mouth at one end and the anus at the other. The head is inconspicuous;

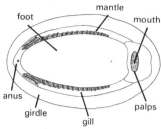

the foot is broad and strong enabling the animal to cling to the most exposed and storm-beaten rocks. A tough, leathery girdle, often decorated with spines, scales or bristles, holds the eight shell segments in place. There are only a few hundred species.

The Scaphopoda or tusk shells, form another small class, unique among molluscs in that their shells, though in one piece, are open at both ends and hollow all the way through. The shells are slightly curved and tapering like an elephant's tusk. They have no eyes, no gills not even a heart. Continuous contractions of the foot which emerges from the wide end of the shell, help to circulate both water and blood through the system. Oxygen is extracted from the water through cells situated in the mantle. They live buried in the sand of the seabed with just the tip of the narrow end of the shell protruding. From this narrow end hundreds of long, hair-like filaments, sticky with mucus, wave around and trap tiny organisms which are then dragged into the mouth.

Cephalopoda, numbering only a few hundred species which include the octopus, the squid and the cuttlefish, is yet the most outstanding class of all invertebrate creatures. They are the most highly evolved, the most intelligent and alert, the fastest moving and among the most successful. They also include the largest of all the molluscs, the giant squid (*Architeuthis*) reaching a length of over seventy feet inclusive.

Cephalopods have brains which are extraordinarily large in proportion to the size of their bodies, highly developed sense organs and large eyes which are remarkably similar in construction to those of humans. In many respects their development, though reached by a quite different branch of the tree of evolution, closely parallels that of the vertebrates.

The nerve fibres of squid are some fifty times larger than those of most animals and allow the swift reaction which accounts for the amazing speed and agility of some species. The nerves of the giant, being over a thousand times thicker than those of humans, have made this great creature one of the most important animals in neurological research.

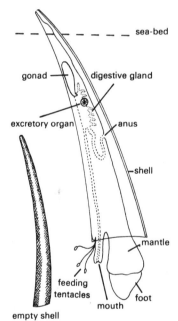

Dentalium, the Tusk Shell. An empty shell is shown on the left. The diagram on the right shows the position the animal takes up in the sand, and the body organs.

An octopus (*Octopus granulatis*) found along the coast of southern Africa. Its arms may reach three feet in length.

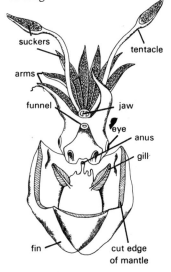

The Squid (*Loligo*) with the body wall cut away.

The mouth of the cephalopod is equipped with horny jaws rather similar in shape to the parrot's beak which are used for biting and killing. The head is encircled by a ring of 'arms' or fleshy tentacles thought to be a modification of the molluscan foot. The octopus has eight of these and the squid ten, including two much longer ones. Each arm has rows of suckers diminishing in size along its length and used for grasping and holding prey. The mantle of the squid has become its main swimming organ, developed into a pair of thick, muscular 'fins' or 'wings' which undulate powerfully. Water trapped in the mantle cavity can be expelled in a forceful jet which propels the animal rapidly in the opposite direction. The squid can squirt water either forwards or backwards so that it can, with equal facility, dart forwards to seize its prey or shoot backwards like a torpedo to escape from danger. Its shell is vestigial, a feather-shaped, horny plate buried deep beneath the mantle. In the cuttlefish it is the tapering piece of softish white calcium known as the cuttle-bone. Only the few species of the genus *Nautilus*, sole remaining descendants of the great class of nautiloids which flourished in Paleozoic seas 300 million years ago, have an external shell.

Another protective device is the cloud of inky substance which cephalopods are able to release into the water to distract their enemies and behind which they may make their escape when danger threatens.

Some species of squid are equipped with patches or spots of luminosity

which give off brilliant rays of opalescent blue and yellow light, sometimes separately and sometimes combined in a dazzling mixture of
sapphire and topaz beams. Another displays flashing lights at the tips of
some of its tentacles.

For rapid colour changes no other creature, not even the chameleon,
can compare with the octopus. Its pigment cells are directly connected
with the nervous system so that colour changes can be made instan-
taneously when danger threatens and the octopus disappears into the
surrounding seascape as if under a cloak of invisibility.

Monoplacophora is the smallest class of all, numbering as yet less
than a dozen species recently discovered living on the ocean floor more
than three miles deep. The first specimens came to light in 1952 when
ten live ones and a few dead shells were dredged from a depth of 11 878
feet off the coast of Mexico by the Danish marine research ship *Galathea*.
The discovery of these 'living fossils', members of a class believed to
have become extinct 350 million years ago, even more ancient and far
more primitive than the coelacanth, is one of the great biological
discoveries of the century.

In appearance, their thin, fragile shells are rather like those of the
limpets, conical in shape with a little tilted peak, semi-transparent and
lined inside with a thin layer of pearly nacre. The largest so far found
are only about an inch and a half across and half an inch high. They
have neither eyes nor tentacles but five pairs of gills surround the
circular foot and their bodies show evidence of segmentation similar

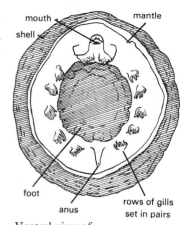

Ventral view of
monoplacophoron *Neopilina*.
Until 1952, this mollusc was
only known from Cambrian
fossils.

Left An octopus taking up a
streamlined position as it
moves away from a rock.
Below left Close-up of the
suckers on one of the two
feeding arms of the squid
(*Loligo forbesi*). The hooked
marginal rings on the suckers
aid in gripping the prey.

to that of the annelid worms and other primitive marine creatures which duplicate the vital organs in each segment.

To withstand the enormous pressure of the water at such depths – several tons to the square inch – these delicate creatures are so constructed as to allow water to permeate every part of their tissue, thus equalizing the pressure within and without.

Perhaps the most outstanding achievement of the molluscs is their success in adapting to life in an amazing range of habitats and their development of specialized forms able to survive under conditions of extraordinary severity and diversity. There are species so sensitive to temperature changes that they are unable to survive outside very narrow limits. The climatic conditions which prevailed in various

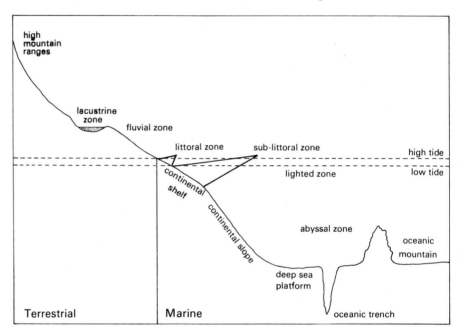

A profile of the environments occupied by molluscs.

parts of the earth thousands of years ago can be verified by the study of such temperature-sensitive snails collected from archaeological sites. In the sea, some species cease to breed if the water temperature falls to a certain level; yet other groups have adapted to almost world-wide distribution covering an extensive range of climate and environment.

Three miles and more above the level of the sea, tiny snails live on lichens among the snowy peaks of high mountains. Three miles and more below the surface of the sea, fragile molluscs live on the ocean floor. Between these limits, which new discoveries may extend at any time, the molluscs have developed species which can meet the challenges that almost every type of environment has to offer.

In the high places of the world, snails have been recorded at over 16 400 feet; they have been found living on juniper bushes at 14 000 feet in the Himalayas and in the Alps at heights where the snow lies for ten months of the year. There are snails in the world's highest lake, Titicaca, 12 550 feet high on the Bolivian plateau. Fourteen species of land snails live in northern Norway well within the Arctic circle and there are freshwater species in northern Siberia where the mean average temperature is below 10°F (−12°C) and the January temperature falls to −30°F (−51°C). Many freshwater snails survive severe winter conditions encased in ice and frozen hard.

A snail crawling across a cactus, testing each thorn before he goes on.

At the other extreme there are snails adapted to life in the desert and midday temperatures of 110°F (43°C), able to survive in such conditions for years at a stretch without either food or water. There are freshwater species too, which live in hot springs and flourish in temperatures ranging from 68 to 122°F (20 to 50°C).

Land molluscs have evolved several ways of coping with the problems of their environment. One of these is the formation of an *epiphragm*, a covering of hardened mucus with which they can seal the aperture of the shell. Thus insulated at the end of the summer season when they are plump and well-fed, such snails are prepared for their winter hibernation. When the temperature falls the snail seeks a hiding place, makes its epiphragm and becomes dormant. The heart almost ceases to beat and the creature sleeps the winter months away. Slugs hibernate too, each coated with a thick layer of its own slime. In tropical lands, during periods of excessive heat, coolness or dryness, snails put themselves into a state of suspended animation known as *aestivation*, in which they remain for several months or until favourable weather returns.

Many incidents have been recorded of snails living dormant for years in the boxes or drawers of collectors' cabinets or even glued on to cards in the old-fashioned manner, and then 'returning to life' if taken out and put into more normal surroundings. The record must be held by the snail kept in a glass-topped box for twenty years, then revived one summer to live a normal life for several months and afterwards put back into its box. That was in 1920. In 1947 the snail was reported to be still alive but dormant, a sleep lasting for forty-seven years apart from those few summer months.

Leaving the mountains, the deserts and the snow, one can find molluscs in every habitat less extreme; snails and slugs in forests, woods and heaths, in every plantation, vegetable patch or garden. All these are gastropods. They live in fresh water too, the pond and river snails are here joined by the bivalves, clams and mussels which have forsaken salt water for fresh.

One of the most successful of the land molluscs is the Great African Snail (*Achatina fulica*) which, unintentionally carried from place to

35

Above *Euglandina*, a cannibal snail of the Everglades, Florida, is about to attack another snail.

Right Showing the body of a snail as it stretches to cross from one leaf to another.

place along with agricultural and horticultural produce, has been spread from its homeland in east Africa to colonize some three fifths of the tropical and subtropical belt of the world. These snails, which grow to seven inches long under favourable conditions, have been famous from the time of Pliny for their fecundity as well as for their size. They are estimated to lay about 600 eggs a year. Buried in the moist earth within reach of banana palms or green plants they flourish exceedingly and, once established, are almost impossible to eradicate.

In 1966 they reached Miami, Florida. Three live snails brought from Hawaii by a schoolboy as a present for his grandmother were not appreciated by that lady and were thrown out. Within a few months their progeny was infesting the gardens of a dozen blocks and seven-inch snails were eating up every bit of greenery in sight. Three years and $30 000 later, the local authority was still fighting to control them.

Down toward the shorelines live the molluscs of the brackish streams and muddy estuaries, of the sea marshes and mangrove swamps, which have learned to take their sea water very much adulterated. Their territory adjoins the first of the sea zones, that of the beaches between the highest tide level and the lowest.

At the top of this littoral zone live gilled marine molluscs which need only an occasional dip in sea water or no more than the salty moisture of sea-spray or spume. In the middle region are species which spend about half their lives under water and the rest in the open air. Down in the seaweed at the level of the lowest tides live a host of molluscs which would die if they were ever exposed to the air for more than an occasional hour or two.

Among the best-known molluscs of the littoral zone are the little periwinkles (*Littorina*) whose many and varied species can be found on every part of the beach. Safely hidden in protective seaweeds the shell may be smooth and thick, coloured in every shade from white and yellow to russet, violet, olive green and brown. On rocks where the waves roll in and out its shell may be rough and tough and spirally grooved; higher up, among the rock pools, the periwinkles are small, coloured grey and brown to match the rocks. At the top of the beach where the waves expend their last energy and splash the rocks at high tide, tiny periwinkles cluster in the crevices. Where there are mangrove trees, large, thin-shelled forms live on the dark roots, coloured to match, while smaller and even more delicate forms live upon the leaves

A tiny gastropod,
Opisthostoma mirabilis
(0.16 inches long), which lives
on limestone outcrops in
northern Borneo.

where their yellow and orange colourings blend with the sunlight filtering through the foliage.

It is in the shallow seas of the continental shelves however, that the richest variety of marine molluscs is to be found. These are the seabeds which slope gently from the shore to a depth of about 400 feet where the steep plunge to the deeps begins. Here there is light and plant life to nourish a host of sea creatures, gastropods, bivalves and tusk shells, octopuses and the small, swift squid which pursue the fish shoals. Here, where the water is warm enough, coral reefs give shelter to the richest variety of molluscs anywhere to be found.

In the abyssal depths which cover nearly two-thirds of the earth's surface, some molluscs have adapted to life in the strange, dark region where no light penetrates and no plant grows, whose denizens must feed on dead matter drifting down, or on each other. This is the home of the giant squid which is the favourite food of the sperm whale. Their indigestible horny beaks lodged in the whales' intestines become coated with a secretion known as ambergris, the precious wax-like substance used to fix perfumes and sometimes found floating after

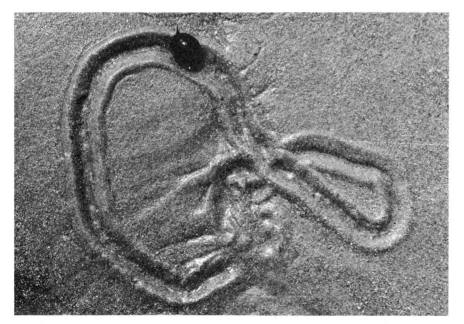

A winkle (*Littorina littoralis*)
maintaining its position on the
shore by changing the
orientation of its movement
in relation to the sun.

The Purple Sea-snail (*Janthina globosa*) and its egg raft.

being evacuated by the whale. Squid have been caught at a depth of 11 000 feet and some of these deep-sea species are so soft and transparent that they could be mistaken for jellyfish. In the upper regions of the abyss many are luminous and some can emit a cloud of luminous blue-green 'ink'. Species of cuttlefish and octopus also make their home in the deep sea and in the ice-cold waters of Antarctica, one species of octopus living at a depth of 9 000 feet.

On the seabed the 'living fossils' are found, survivors of primitive molluscs whose contemporaries became extinct many millions of years ago. Such are the rare and valuable slit shells (*Pleurotomaria*) so highly prized by collectors, the recently-discovered gastroverms and the Pearly Nautilus (*Nautilus pompilius*).

Some 100 species of molluscs are pelagic and spend their lives afloat in the open sea. Such are the delicate pteropods, small, transparent 'sea-butterflies' which flutter through the water on undulating 'wings'. Some of the tropical species have tiny shells, cone-shaped, triangular or spiral. Best known of the pelagic molluscs is the Purple Sea-snail (*Janthina*) whose frail, violet-tinted shell is sometimes tossed intact upon the shore. *Janthina* spends its life afloat, suspended upside down from a raft of bubbles to which some species attach their egg capsules.

Some molluscs have found strange dwelling places. Piddocks (*Pholas*) and date mussels (*Lithophaga*) excavate burrows for themselves in soft rocks such as limestone and sandstone, or in coral. The shipworm (*Teredo*), which is a bivalve mollusc not a worm, tunnels into wood. The cup-and-saucer molluscs (*Cheila*) and the little conical *Calyptrea* live inside the dead shells of larger species and shape themselves to the curves of their adopted homes. Tiny parasitic molluscs such as *Stylifer* live embedded in the flesh of starfish or nestle in the angles of their 'arms'; while *Eulima* live in sea-cucumbers and sea urchins.

In common with all other living organisms, the most vital urge of every mollusc is the need to propagate. Every other activity is basically directed to this end: the continuation of the species.

It is believed that originally all molluscs cast their eggs and sperm into the sea, as the bivalves do today, leaving fertilization, distribution

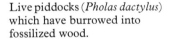

Live piddocks (*Pholas dactylus*) which have burrowed into fossilized wood.

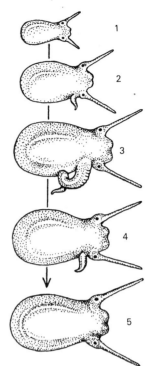

and survival to the vagaries of the currents, the tides and the chance evasion of predators. By this method, thousands of eggs must be released to ensure that a few will survive. It has been estimated that a female oyster may produce three million eggs in a single season, out of which only a tiny fraction have a chance of reaching adulthood.

After fertilization, the eggs of many molluscs hatch into *trochophore* larvae. These change very rapidly into *veliger*, tiny free-swimming creatures which for a time join the plankton and become part of the food supply of a multitude of sea creatures, from tiny fish to the huge baleen whale.

Many are the methods evolved by molluscs to improve their chances of survival. *Patella* limpets breed after stormy weather when strong winds and waves will disperse their eggs widely. The 'Coon Oyster (*Ostrea frons*) releases its eggs into the first very high tide after a full moon. The eggs of the European Flat Oyster (*Ostrea edulis*) are fertilized within the female by sperm drawn in with the water.

To ensure an adequate supply of both sperm and eggs, oysters alternate their sex throughout life, functioning first as males and then as females which, after releasing their eggs, change back to males.

Whelks (*Buccinum*) in common with most marine snails, are separately sexed, the male having a large, muscular penis situated behind and to the right of the head. The female encloses her eggs in protective capsules, each of which may contain as many as 3 000 eggs of which only a tiny fraction, about half of one per cent, will develop. All the rest merely provide nourishment for the lucky few which will crawl out of the capsules as fully formed baby whelks.

Snails which move around on seabed or shore have a better chance of finding a mate than the sedentary types. These have to work out alternative methods of ensuring that a member of the opposite sex will be at hand when required. None has solved this problem more ingeniously than the American Slipper Limpet (*Crepidula fornicata*), well-known in British waters as a highly unwelcome immigrant which causes devastation in the oyster beds and has flourished so mightily

Left Two clumps of Slipper Limpets (*Crepidula fornicata*) attached to a stone. On the left is an empty shell.
Above The Slipper Limpet, showing sex reversal. The shell has been removed. 1 Immature male, 2 Developing male, 3 Mature male, 4 Degenerating male (penis atrophies), 5 Animal becomes female.

The egg collar of the Moon Snail (*Natica catena*).

that in some areas it reaches a density of up to 100 tons per acre. They live in clumps of ten or a dozen individuals, squatting one on top of another. Clumps join on to clumps and become chains. In each clump, the molluscs at the bottom are females and those at the top males. In between will usually be found some which are in the process of changing sex from male to female. All start life as males. A young male settling on the top of a clump has an elongated penis which can reach the females below. The females below release a hormone which keeps the males male; but when a female gets old or dies so that the supply of hormone diminishes, males above begin to change sex and the birth of the next generation is ensured.

Cephalopods, the octopus and squid, are also usually of separate sexes and the females are often much larger and more numerous than the males. During the mating season the small male octopus courts his chosen female with a dazzling display of colour changes and caresses her with his many arms. One of these is modified to form a sex organ which, laden with sperm, can be inserted into the female. In the case of the *Argonauta* the arm of the male is detached and left within the mantle cavity of the female. This is the female octopus which makes a delicate shell of exquisite beauty as a cradle for her eggs and swims with it clasped in her arms. She dies soon after the young have hatched.

Most land snails and also the sea slug and sea hares, are hermaphrodite, combining complete sets of both male and female sex organs in each individual and producing both eggs and sperm from separate ducts. They are able to fertilize themselves but much prefer to exchange sperm with a partner. The Edible Snails (*Helix pomatia*) for example, make love with much rubbing together of the soles of their gliding 'feet' and caress each other with the tips of their extended tentacles. As passion rises they stab each other with sharp 'love darts' and lock themselves together in a tight embrace. After this, mating takes place and each stores the sperm of the other in its body until its own eggs are ready for fertilization. The Great Grey Slugs (*Limax maximus*) take to the air to do their courting. They mate in mid-air, dangling at the end of a strong thread of mucus suspended from the branch of a tree.

For some molluscs the duties of reproduction are finished once their eggs have been cast into the water, but many others take care of their eggs and sometimes of their young. Marine snails lay their eggs in protective capsules and often attach these to rocks, stone or rubble. The moon snail (*Polinices*) makes a 'collar' of sand grains bound with mucus and attaches her eggs to the inner side. The female cowry lays her egg cluster in a secluded niche in the coral and sits brooding on them concealed beneath her extended foot.

Snails of the exposed inter-tidal rocks such as *Trochus* incubate their eggs in a special 'nursery chamber' within the mother's shell and some of the boring clams keep their young inside the burrow until they are old enough to start boring their own holes. The mother octopus fixes her eggs in strings to the roof of her cave and stays on guard, waving her arms to keep fresh water circulating around them.

The continued existence of molluscs over so many millions of years is evidence of their tenacity and proficiency. Some species are under pressure in certain localities and many species of land snails are threatened by extinction due to the activities of man. But the vast majority continue, as yet, to survive and flourish.

In some species the sex can be distinguished by the formation of the shell. Above left: a female helmet shell (*Cassis cornuta*) which can reach 14 inches in length. Above right: the male, much smaller, with fewer but larger knobs on the shoulder. Below: spider shells (*Lambis lambis*) from the Sulu sea where sex differences are striking; the male (on the left) is richly marked and not much more than half the size of the female (right) whose projecting spines are long and up-curling.

The Coveted Ones

There are not many species of molluscs with very large shells and few of these are rare, but all the big, handsome univalve shells commonly known as conchs have long been coveted by man. In early times they were used as trumpets, symbols of royalty and libation vessels; and continue to be so used in parts of the world today.

For the modern collector these showy specimens add interest and colour as well as the beauty of their shapes, to his shelves and cabinets. They are also desired by many people who have no interest in shells in general, simply because they are large and beautiful and ornamental and people like to have them around.

Such are the great helmet shells (*Cassis*), many of which were first brought to Europe as ballast in the holds of sailing ships; the Sacred Chank Shell of India (*Turbinella pyrum*), the many-fingered spider shells (*Lambis*), the lamp shells (*Bursa*), Triton's Trumpet (*Charonia tritonis*) of the Indo-Pacific and the flaring-lipped *Strombus* conchs of the West Indies.

Many tropical shells which were considered extremely rare and valuable by early collectors were only rare in their times because so few had reached the west and so little was known about them. One species which had an extraordinary appeal for eighteenth-century collectors was the Hammer Oyster (*Malleus malleus*) which is shaped like a great 'T', the hinge forming the crossbar projecting on either side. Inside, the shell is black with a patch of dark, iridescent nacre at the spot where the body of the animal lay. The extraordinary shape of this shell must have been its chief attraction and Dutch collectors who liked to have their portraits painted standing beside their cabinets or tables of shells and other curiosities, took care to have the Hammer Oyster conspicuously displayed or held in the hand. At a sale in Holland in 1792, a 'large black polish hammer, the handle six the cross eight inches long' (*Malleus malleus*), was sold for thirty-two guilders. Another which came from Manila and was described as being of the greatest beauty and rarity and of unique size, measuring nearly nine inches from point to point, was sold by auction in 1821 for five guineas. Today it would be worth but a few shillings. It is a common shell, found in shallow water near coral reefs where it clings by its byssus threads and is often so thickly covered with seaweed, algae and other marine growths that it is not easily seen.

A more delicate and less common species, the White Hammer (*Malleus albus*) was also greatly prized and regarded as 'very rare'. A specimen in the Duchess of Portland's collection, described as having been brought from New Holland (Australia) by Captain Cook, was sold for four guineas in 1786, a great deal of money in those days. So greatly in demand was this species in Holland that fakes were made and many of the shells displayed so proudly were false.

The Precious Wentletrap or Staircase Shell (*Epitonium scalare*) is so exquisitely formed that it is no wonder the early collectors valued it above rubies and paid prices for which it might have been copied in gold and studded with diamonds. The tapering spiral whorls of this small, dainty shell which reaches not much more that two inches in length, are not sutured together as is the case with most spiral univalves. There is a space between them all the way from the nucleus to the aperture and the whole is covered with very regular and ridge-like varices which have the appearance of a white latticework cage enclosing the glossy whorls, or the treads of a spiral staircase.

At the height of their popularity these shells would fetch several hundred pounds apiece. The Emperor Francis I, husband of Maria Theresa, paid 4 000 guilders for one. They held pride of place in the cabinets of the Empress Catherine of Russia and the Queen of Sweden. Though no longer considered rare, they are still greatly admired and fine specimens as much coveted as ever, but their prices nowadays are a modest fraction of those of earlier times.

There were other coveted rarities which did not in fact exist, such as the fabulous 'Matchless Cone' (*Conus cedonulli*). Many collectors believed themselves to possess this treasure. One was bought in 1731 by the King of Portugal for over a thousand livres, another for nearly a thousand Dutch florins by a dealer, who offered it to the King of Denmark as being unique, having no equal in the whole of Europe. The Duchess of Portland tried to buy one for a hundred pounds but the owner wanted three times as much. No two of these appeared to be exactly alike, so each owner believed his specimen to be the unique, the one-and-only Matchless Cone. In fact, *Conus cedonulli* was a composite of several variable species.

Such legends die hard, especially when good money has been paid. The Matchless Cones continued to be sought after, and were eagerly snapped up – though at much lower prices – during the next century. One actually appeared in the sale list of a New York auction as late as 1962. It was probably *Conus dominicanus* and sold for US$17.

A shell which does exist but which is of little interest to modern collectors is that of the Glassy Nautilus (*Carinaria cristata*), once believed to be as rare and valuable as the Matchless Cone. It is extremely delicate and fragile, as if made from the finest spun glass, shaped like a pixie's cap with the point tilted to the side and ending in a tiny coil. It was thought to be the shell of a cephalopod similar to the *Argonauta*, hence its popular name, but it is actually that of a pelagic snail, a heteropod which lives in the open sea. The first specimen recorded in Europe in 1754 came from Amboina in the Dutch East Indies. It was four inches long. In 1796 it was sold for 300 guilders and thirty years later re-sold for almost twice as much. Believed to be the rarest of all shells, it was thought that only a very few existed. In Paris a good specimen could be sold for several thousand livres. Not much more than a hundred years later a 'very perfect' specimen fetched only £3.

One shell above all others became the best known to the man-in-the-street and the most sought after by modern collectors: the famous cone shell, Glory-of-the-Sea (*Conus gloriamaris*). Until September, 1969, it was believed to be one of the rarest shells in the world. It is one of the few shells which has made 'front-page' news. It has been made the central theme of a book; has been stolen from a museum; and has changed hands at some of the highest prices ever paid for individual shells.

Conus dominicanus (approx. 2 inches long), one of several variable species sold as the legendary Matchless Cone (*Conus cedonulli*).

43

Two views of the famous
Glory-of-the-Sea Cone
(*Conus gloriamaris,* this
specimen 5 inches long)
stolen from the American
Museum of Natural History
and never recovered.

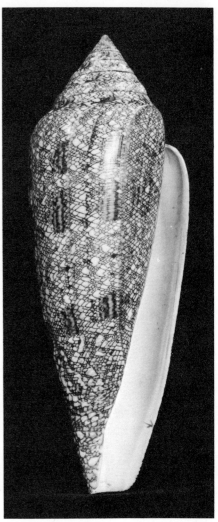

It is a beautiful, tapering shell, covered with delicate 'tent' markings in fawn to russet colouring on a creamy ground, but few would give it the first prize for either elegance or beauty. It is not even particularly distinctive and several other species of cone, especially the quite common Textile Cone (*Conus textile*) have been hopefully mistaken for it.

Such is its fame that many legends have grown up around it. For example, the story of the famous collector who, possessing one specimen which he believed to be unique, paid an enormous price for a second one which turned up at an auction and immediately set his foot upon it and crushed it to pieces. The reef on which the only two known live specimens had been found was reported to have disappeared during an earthquake. *C. gloriamaris* was assumed to have become extinct and its few known shells therefore, all the more valuable. Collectors have been said to turn faint at the very sight of this marvel and to have been so shaken by emotion that they feared to hold such fragile treasure in their hands.

The first specimen of which we have mention appeared in the catalogue of an auction sale in 1757. No one knew where it came from, no one knew who had given it the splendid title of 'Glory-of-the-Sea', but this name was officially perpetuated when Chemnitz described and named this same shell in 1777. Fifty years later, in 1837, the first two live specimens were collected by Hugh Cuming (see page 183) on an island north of Mindanao in the southern Philippines, and his discovery was widely reported when the news reached Europe and America.

Only a very few specimens were then known to collectors, but diligent searches through old and forgotten collections and the occasional exciting 'find' in a junk shop or on a market stall, kept interest alive. Most of these chance-found treasures were beach-worn, chipped, damaged and in poor condition, yet they commanded fabulous prices.

So well-known had the shell become that the Victorian novelist Francesca M. Steele who wrote under the pseudonym Darley Dale, published a book in 1887 called *The Glory of the Sea* in which the theft and recovery of the shell form the central theme. It is really an introduction to conchology disguised as a novel, combining instruction with entertainment, a favourite Victorian literary device.

More than a century after Cuming's find, only a couple of dozen of these shells were known. They were so valuable and so coveted that in 1951 an exhibit in the American Museum of Natural History was broken into and a very fine specimen stolen, which has never been recovered. In 1957 one shell sold for US $2 000.

More dead shells in varying condition began to turn up in New Guinea, New Britain and the Solomon Islands, often washed ashore after storms. In the 1960s even small, beach-worn specimens were fetching around US $100 and perfect ones as much as US $700.

Then, late in 1969, came the stunning news that a 'large number' of live *C. gloriamaris* had been found by aqualung divers working off the north coast of Guadalcanal. The divers had stumbled upon a whole colony while actually looking for the habitat of a rare cowry. Over the following months they collected over 120 specimens in the same area.

The story of the Glory-of-the-Sea Cone has been given in some detail because it offers the classic and best-known example of the fluctuating fortunes of a 'rare' shell. Its story underlines the question: 'What is rarity?' and the folly of buying 'rare' shells.

Rare creatures may be those which are rare in nature, of which very few individuals exist. They may be those which are difficult, dangerous or expensive to obtain and of which, therefore, very few specimens are available. Others may be considered rare simply because their habitats have not been discovered.

Some of the habitats of *C. gloriamaris* are now known. There may well be others and even more of these lovely shells will come to the hands of museums and collectors. It might have been thought that the influx of new specimens would result in a drop in the shell's appeal, but this has not happened. The old shells, cherished over so many years, are often poor and damaged specimens. Even when perfect, few have accurate data – the precise information relating to the locality and circumstances of their finding – which is of prime importance to the serious collector and enhances the value of the shell. The newly found specimens have this added attraction and modern collectors, ever more scientifically minded, still covet these gems for their cabinets and are willing to pay handsomely for them. A hundred or so specimens among thousands of collectors goes nowhere near satisfying the demand.

Of all the shells prized and treasured by man, the cowries must surely hold pride of place. Primitive humans held them in awe and veneration for their supposed magical qualities (see chapter five) and counted them among their most cherished possessions. They have been found in ancient treasure hoards and burial sites all over the world and they are valued today in many primitive societies as symbols of status or lucky charms.

During historical times certain small varieties have been sought in their billions for use as currency (see chapter six). To shell collectors of the last few centuries, cowries have always headed the popularity poll. Almost every collector has wished to include a tray of these shining gems in his cabinet and the truly rare ones are the most coveted shells in the world.

The best known and one of the largest and handsomest is the Tiger Cowry (*Cypraea tigris*) which is not striped like the tiger, as one would imagine from its name, but richly spotted like the leopard. It inhabits the Indo-Pacific regions where it is common and easily found in quite shallow water. Large numbers were brought to Europe as souvenirs by seamen serving in ships trading with the East and they could be seen and admired on many a cottage mantelpiece.

The cowry which became the most coveted shell of all time, however, is the rare Golden Cowry (*Cypraea aurantium*) which, for centuries before it had been either seen or heard of in Europe, had been worn in the regalia of the kings of Fiji and as a badge of rank by certain noblemen and chieftains. Polynesian peoples who obtained specimens by barter looked upon them as their most treasured magical objects, to be handed down as heirlooms. The typical form is about four inches long, the dome a brilliant golden orange and highly glossy, the base creamy white. There are other specimens which have grown larger and are of a more pinkish tint.

Captain Cook and his men were the first Europeans to see these gorgeous shells when they called at the Fijian Islands during his second voyage to the South Seas. Specimens brought back by the scientists and seamen of the expedition were seen in England during the 1770s. These had been obtained from the natives of Fiji and usually had holes bored through the shell ready for hanging from a cord as a chest ornament. At the beginning of the nineteenth century, specimens of good quality were worth from £10 to £20 apiece and although their values have fluctuated greatly with the rise and fall of interest in shell collecting, in the second half of this century they have become more popular than ever, fetching over £20 each and sometimes quite exorbitant prices such as the 880 francs paid at a Paris sale in 1967 and the £55 paid for a pierced shell of poor quality at a Sotheby's auction in 1968.

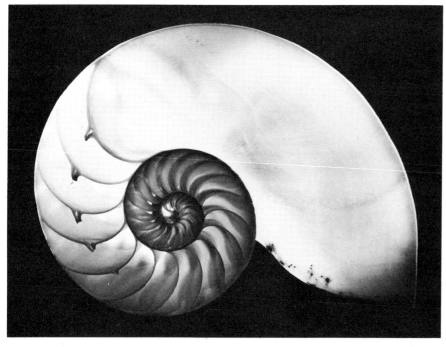

Left Strombus listeri (6 inches long), up to a few years ago, was one of the rarest of the Strombus shells.
Below Sectioned, Chambered Nautilus (*Nautilus pompilius*, 6 inches long).

Tibia martinii (6 inches long), first discovered in the Philippines, in the late nineteenth century, is still fairly rare.

A register kept by the Hawaiian Malacological Society listed, up to June 1970, a total of 294 specimens including broken and eroded specimens as well as good ones. More have been found since then, including a haul of seventeen from an atoll in the Marshall Islands. For long, their habitat remained a secret but it is now known that they prefer to live deep in caves well down on the seaward side of reefs which take the full force of wind and wave. The scuba divers can get there at slack tide in calm weather, but they cannot always reach the cowries.

The Pearly or Chambered Nautilus (*Nautilus pompilius*) has long been famed for the wonderful symmetry of its lovely shell in which the growth-form of the logarithmic spiral seems to find its perfect expression. In the shell of the nautilus the spiral increases its diameter exactly three times in each complete turn, forming a coiled tube of many chambers which cannot be studied in all its intricacy until the shell has been cut through lengthwise.

The shell is thin and smooth, white on the outside and streaked across with bands of chestnut brown. The inside is lined throughout with pearly nacre which, on the earlier whorls, has exactly the shade and lustre of burnished silver. The animal, as it grows, makes for itself a continuing series of chambers, each progressively larger than the one before. Each vacated chamber is sealed off from the next by a delicate wall of pearl curved to duplicate in miniature the main spiral of the shell. In the centre of each wall is a small hole, sunk from the outer side and again most delicately curved. This is the septa and the soft cord of flesh known as the siphuncle passes through each one like a 'tail'. This connects the animal in the outermost chamber with all the inner ones and is used in adjusting water and gas pressures within.

The animal which forms this marvel of nature is a cephalopod, one of a tiny group of unique creatures, sole survivors in the modern world of the great nautiloid family which was making evolutionary history 400 million years ago and which has left 10 000 species in the fossil record (see page 11).

The early silvery whorls, cut to an inch or so in diameter and worn so as to display the curved hole of the septal neck have been for centuries highly prized head ornaments in Samoa and other islands of the

Above The Precious Wentletrap or Staircase Shell (*Epitonium scalare* 2 inches long) was at one time the most highly prized of shells.

Left The common Black Hammer Oyster (*Malleus malleus*, 8 inches long) and the smaller and rarer White Hammer (*Malleus albus*).

South Pacific. In the West, the complete shell has always been a collector's favourite, especially if a second one, carefully sectioned, can be displayed beside it. Eighteenth-century collectors in Holland would pay 100 guilders for a nautilus shell richly carved and engraved.

By virtue of size alone the shell of the Giant Clam (*Tridacna gigas*) is one of the most famous. The Giant Clam is the largest by far of all the shelled molluscs and it is famed not only for its size but for its long standing reputation as a 'man-killer' (see page 140). The largest specimen recorded came from Sumatra and measured four feet six inches in length and weighed 507 pounds. An Australian specimen weighed $579\frac{1}{2}$ pounds but its length is not known.

Giant Clams live in the shallow water of tropical seas, lying on coral reefs with the hinge downward and the undulating edges of the great valves held upwards. Unlike most other bivalves, they are hermaphrodite and produce both eggs and sperm. They obtain most of their food by 'farming' vast numbers of tiny marine plants in special 'gardens' located along the edges of their mantles which are exposed to water and light as soon as the valves are opened. No one knows how long they live though it has been estimated that their life span may well cover several centuries.

The Bajau people – strange sea-gypsies of the Sulu Sea who spend their lives afloat, sailing with the monsoon winds from north-east to south-west and back again – believe that the 'lands of the Kima' (Giant Clam) belong to them. They mean the great coral reefs which only become 'land' for a few brief hours at low tide and on which only the Bajau set foot. At one time they laid claim to some of the birds' nest caves on the mainland of Borneo simply because fossil Giant Clams had been found in them.

The first shells of the huge mollusc brought to Europe caused a sensation and were considered gifts fit for royalty (see page 180). John Evelyn, the diarist, saw a pair in a Paris grotto in 1649 and was told by the owner that he had paid 200 crowns for them in Amsterdam. Although not rare (except for those of record size) they must always command a good price because of the labour involved in getting them and the high cost of transport.

The rare shells of today, those most coveted by collectors, are chiefly those of molluscs which live in deep water and can be obtained only by difficult and expensive deep-sea dredging requiring special apparatus, from deep trawling and from the stomachs of bottom-feeding fish. The most sought after by collectors come from depths of up to 300 fathoms (1 800 feet). Those from still greater depths become progressively smaller, more delicate and colourless and make less of a display in the cabinet. These are of greater interest to the scientist than to shell collectors in general.

Since man has begun to explore the depths of the sea it has been discovered that certain groups of creatures, unable to respond to the challenges of life near the shore, have not become extinct as had been believed, but have taken refuge in the deeps. For them evolutionary time has stood still and they have survived there virtually unchanged throughout the millennia. The abyssal depths are, indeed, the last refuge of the 'living fossil'.

Such are the gastroverm (see page 33), the nautilus and also the slit shells (*Pleurotomaria*) whose last survivors were believed to have become extinct at least sixty-five million years ago after an evolutionary history stretching back 500 million years.

The slit shells are very primitive gastropods, ancestral forms of the

Rumpf's Slit Shell (*Entemnotrochus rumphii*, 7½ inches long) is the largest of the slit shells.

top shells and turban shells of today. They are distinguished by a narrow slit which cuts back from the outer lip of the aperture along the middle of the whorl. As the shell grows, the mollusc prolongs the slit but fills in the earlier parts, leaving a continuous spiral scar along the whorls. The shell, usually rather thin, is lined with iridescent nacre.

Until 1856 these gastropods, were known only from fossils. Then a French naval officer serving in the Lesser Antilles, obtained a small slit shell from a fish trap. It was dead and inhabited by a hermit crab, but its discovery caused a sensation among conchologists. This was subsequently named *Perotrochus quoyanus* and was eventually acquired by the British Museum in 1941.

A second slit shell, of another species, *Entemnotrochus adansonianus* was found six years later and, as so often happens when the hunt is on, other species began to turn up in the most unexpected places. One was found in a shellcraft workshop in Japan, while another species, now known to live in the deep waters of the China Sea, turned up in a shell-dealer's basket of miscellaneous shells in Rotterdam. This was *E. rumphii*, the largest species yet discovered, reaching about eight inches in length.

About a dozen species are now known and live specimens collected with great difficulty command prices ranging from about £20 to several hundred pounds according to quality and rarity. They appear to be widely distributed but most species have been found in the area of the Caribbean and in the waters of Japan and the North China Sea.

The Japanese fishermen who keep a sharp watch for them in their deep-water trawls, called them 'millionaire shells' when they found that collectors would pay such high prices for them. The most common Japanese species, *Pleurotomaria hirase* is usually known as the Emperor's

Personal choice – a selection of favourite species collected by the author in Sabah, North Borneo. Key: 1 *Strombus vittatus vittatus* 2 *Distorsio anus* 3 *Tibia melanostoma*, this specimen 6 inches long 4 *Babylonia ambulacrum* 5 *Lambis scorpius* 6 *Mactra violacea* 7 *Cypraea argus* 8 *Cymatium rhinoseros* 9 *Tonna dolium* (form *parvula*) 10 *Hydatina zonata* 11 *Cymatium clandestinum* 12 *Oliva cryptospira* 13 *Stellaria solaris* 14 *Cypraea cribraria* 15 *Conus characteristicus* 16 *Natica fluctuata* 17 *Conus nobilis* (form *cordigera*) 18 *Vexillum filiareginae* 19 *Pterynotus triqueter* 20 *Terebra pertusa* 21 *Cypraea stolida* 22 *Natica onca* 23 *Cypraea punctata* 24 *Peristernia incarnata* 25 *Cypraea ursellus* 26 *Dolicholatirus lancea.*

Large, handsome shells are ever popular for display. Key: 1 Yellow Helmet (*Cassis cornuta*, this specimen 10 inches long) 2 Giant Spider Conch (*Lambis truncata*) 3 Chambered Nautilus (*Nautilus pompilius*) 4 Cross section of same 5 Giant Tun Shell (*Tonna olearium*) 6 Frilly Clam (*Tridacna squamosa*) 7 Spider Conch (*Lambis chiragra*) 8 Imperial Volute (*Voluta imperialis*).

Top Shell in honour of Hirohito, Emperor of Japan, a keen marine biologist and owner of one of the finest private shell collections in the world.

Among the most sought-after shells of today are the Glory-of-India Cone (*Conus milneedwardsi*) and the Great Spotted Cowry (*Cypraea guttata*).

The discovery of *C. milneedwardsi* (which used to be called *C. clytospira*) was considered to be one of the great conchological 'finds' of the late nineteenth century although it had been known over a century earlier when it was called the 'Drap d'Or Pyramidal' or 'Cloth of Gold Pyramid'. It is still one of the rarest and most beautiful of the cones, remarkable for its supremely elegant and slender shape and for its unusually narrow and elongated spire. It reaches a length of six inches and is boldly patterned in rich chestnut brown and white.

The specimens collected in the 1890s by F. W. Townsend aroused considerable interest. He specialized in collecting molluscs from encrusted submarine telegraph cables, from which he obtained many new and rare species. One specimen collected near Bombay in 1903 is now in the National Museum of Wales; another large one was discovered in a fish basket in Mauritius (1930s); but by the early 1960s less than a dozen specimens were known. It has been a far rarer shell than *C. gloriamaris* and many think it far handsomer, yet it has never been so well known. In the later 1960s, however, new specimens began to be taken alive by deep trawling from a depth of 150 fathoms off Mozambique, East Africa. Three live-taken juveniles and a dead and

Above The rare Glory of India Cone (*Conus milneedwardsi*). This specimen is 3¾ inches long and was collected off the Bombay coast in 1903.
Right The Aulica Volute (*Aulica aulica*, 3–5 inches long) is no longer rare but is still one of the most prized volutes.

The Sun Shell (*Astraea heliotropium*, 3 inches diameter) brought from New Zealand by Captain Cook, was a highly prized shell in the eighteenth century.

damaged adult shell were obtained from a prawn-fishing trawler and later sold in the United States for a sum of $2 400. More specimens are being found in the same area and it may one day become available, like the Glory-of-the-Sea, to more than the very wealthiest of collectors.

It is a sad commentary on man's greed however, that once the habitat of such coveted molluscs has been discovered, unscrupulous (and sometimes merely ignorant) collectors are prepared to damage or destroy that habitat in order to gather the treasure more quickly. Even explosives have been used in some cases.

The Great Spotted Cowry (*Cypraea guttata*) is one of the most striking and unusual of all the cowries. If it were as common as the Tiger Cowry it would still be a coveted shell. Its white spots against an orange-tawny ground are not unusual, for many species are spotted. In this species the 'teeth' are unique. They are prolonged in raised lines of a rich brown right across the creamy base, up and over the sides and the tips of the shell to merge into the smooth dome, so that the shell looks as if it had been decorated with fine pipings of chocolate icing.

It was first described in 1791 and until 1963 only sixteen specimens were known. A specimen sold by auction in 1818 from the collection of H. C. Jennings and now in the British Museum, was at that time the only one known in England. In 1963 a specimen found in the Solomon Islands was sold for US$2 000 and in the following year the largest specimen yet discovered, about two and three quarter inches in length, was collected in the Moluccas. In recent years a dozen or more additional specimens have been found in localities as far apart as Japan and the New Hebrides and these are now bringing around US$500 apiece.

Even rarer is the Prince Cowry (*Cypraea valentia*), still one of the rarest of all cowries. It is a plump, bulbous shell, rather hump-backed, with dark brown spots on its flanks and a large patch of irregular brown markings on either side of the dome. The white tips of the shell are outlined by several sharp, dark lines which might have been drawn by a fine pen. So little was known about it that it used to be called the 'Brindled Cowry of the Persian Gulf' though its habitat has now been discovered to be in the South Pacific around the island of New Britain and Guadalcanal in the Solomons. A specimen auctioned in 1865 for £40 was described as being one of only four known specimens. The first discovered in this century was a dead shell, but in very good

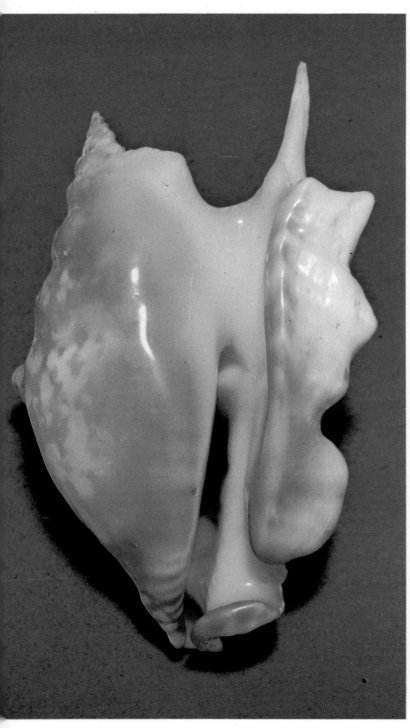

Above *Strombus taurus*
(4 inches long) was a rare shell.
Good specimens are still
highly valued.
Right *Murex elongatus* ($3\frac{1}{2}$
inches long) is a rare shell
which is greatly prized due to
its unusual shape.

Left *Lyria lyraeformis*
(4 inches long) is a much
coveted shell.
Above *Harpa costata*
(4 inches long) was once
considered a rarity and is still
highly prized.

A thorny oyster (*Spondylus petroselineum*, 3 inches across) one of the collector's favourites among the bivalves.

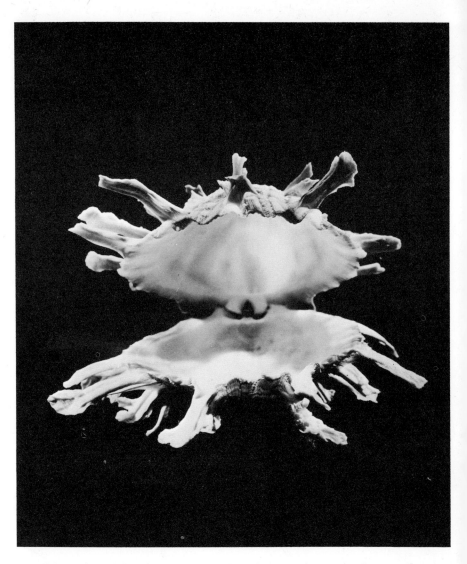

condition, found in 1966 on a coral reef somewhere on the north coast of New Britain. *C. valentia* is a deep-water species and only by some extraordinary chance does a dead shell reach a reef or a shore. Such shells would be worth around £500.

The volutes are also among the most coveted of shells, partly on account of their outstandingly vivid colours and markings and also because, out of some 200 known species, a large proportion rank as 'uncommon' and over two dozen are so rare that they are known from only one or two specimens. These are the species which live at very great depths.

The Imperial Volute (*Voluta imperialis*), a large, heavy shell with rings of sharp prongs like the spikes of a crown, is not uncommon but it is not easy to find a really large specimen, eight or nine inches long, in perfect condition. As the animal ages, the points of the prongs tend to become damaged or eroded. Another much sought after is the Noble Volute (*V. nobilis*) with its bold brown markings and variety of shadings. The truly rare volutes, however, few collectors can hope to acquire. These are such as the superb *V. bednalli* of Australia, marked with a most regular all-over design in black and white; and the fabulous *Cymbiola cymbiola*, so rare that it was not found again after the eighteenth century until trawlers began bringing specimens to light off the southeast coast of Bali Island, Indonesia, in 1972.

The murex shells must be mentioned too, for their eye-catching arrangements of spikes and spines have made them always attractive to man. One of the most striking, *Murex pecten*, has long been known in the West as the Comb-of-Venus and in the East as the Comb-of-Allah. It is not rare, as is the much-coveted and very rare Alabaster Murex (*Murex alabaster*) of Japan whose spines are decorated with fluted frills of incredible delicacy.

Another very popular group is that of the spindle shells (*Tibia*), all uncommon and some very rare. These long, pointed shells have short finger-like projections spaced around the outer edge of the lip. The most striking have a very long and slender siphonal canal which doubles the length of the shell.

On the whole, bivalves are not popular and few are coveted except for the pectens or scallops which can be found in such brilliant colours, clear and strong – yellow, orange, purple; subtle shades of pink and lilac; pure white and deepest brown – and the thorny oysters (*Spondylus*), so greatly prized by the prehistoric peoples of Europe (see page 16) and by the collector of today.

Among the land snails the only widely coveted ones have been the colourful tree-snails of tropical forests, especially the lovely Green Tree Snails (*Papustyla pulcherrima*) of Manus Island, Admiralty Islands, which are one of the few molluscs with shells of a true, clear, leaf-green colour. So great has been the demand for these green shells that the species is in danger of extinction. Many are collected by timbermen as a profitable sideline to tree-felling. In the United States this species is now listed as 'endangered' and it is illegal to import specimens either dead or alive.

Murex shells collected by the author in Sabah, North Borneo. Key: 1 *Murex ramosus* (this specimen 8 inches long) 2 *Murex torrefactus* 3 *Murex cichoreus* 4 *Murex ternispina* 5 and 6 *Murex nigrospinosus* 7 *Homalocantha zamboi* 8 *Murex bruneus* 9 *Murex scorpius* 10 *Murex bipinnatus* 11 *Murex haustellum* 12 *Murex mindanaoensis* 13 *Murex brevispina*.

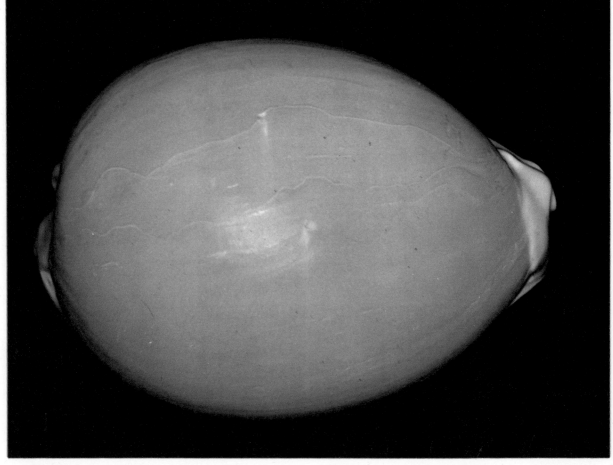

Far left above The Green Tree Snail (*Papustyla pulcherrima*) from Manus Island, Admiralty Islands, is one of the few non-marine species generally coveted by collectors.

Far left below The Golden Cowry (*Cypraea aurantium*, 3–5 inches long) is one of the most consistently prized of all the shells.

Left *Voluta bednalli* (up to 6 inches). This rare shell is considered by many to be the most beautiful and striking of the volutes.

Magic, Mythology and Religion

Beliefs in the magical properties of shells are worldwide and most likely originated with the first man to pick up a cowry on the shores of the Red Sea and to discern, in the shape, colour and form of its aperture, a fancied resemblance to the sexual parts of woman, the door through which a precious child enters the world. The manner in which the animal extrudes itself from the lips of the shell reminded him also of the act of parturition.

Two basic needs dominated the life of early man; the need to find food and the need for children to perpetuate his race. His reasoning led him to believe that an object which appeared to resemble a part of the human body could magically influence that part, and that the object itself possessed vital and magical powers.

The cowry, therefore, was believed to have the power of conferring fertility, to be a protection against sterility and to increase sexual potency. It was the repository of the vital principle or 'soul substance', the ensurer of life and of resurrection, which is life's continuance. It became the symbol of womanhood, the source of life, dwelling place of the deity who made fertile both the women and the crops and the murmur of whose voice could be heard in the shell. Such shells have been found among the most prized possessions of primitive peoples all over the world. No other objects have been so widely revered.

Hump-back Cowry (*Cypraea mauritiana* 3½ inches) showing aperture.

Triton shell trumpet from Fiji.

So the shell of the cowry, with its power of ensuring fertility and easy delivery was hung as near as possible to the reproductive parts, on aprons or girdles, and became regarded as the most suitable gift to be presented to girls when they reached puberty or when they married. Barren women would wear them in hope and pregnant ones in confidence. As clothing came to be used, shells and shell amulets tended to become more and more decorative.

Man is often dominated by fears; fears of death, disease and the supernatural; of malevolent spirits; of black magic and most of all of the 'evil eye', or of being 'overlooked' by an ill-disposed person. Such looks might strike a man with weakness or disease, might cause sterility or even death. The best protections were amulets or charms chosen for their likeness to vital parts of the body; of all these, the cowry was by far the most powerful and important, especially as a second resemblance was perceived between the slit of the cowry shell fringed with its 'teeth' and the half-closed human eye fringed with its lashes.

Many of the magical powers of the cowry came to be transferred to other shells; to the large tritons and conchs which could be made into the trumpets through which the gods spoke; to the ear shells (*Haliotis*) which resemble the human ear; to snail shells of many kinds; and especially those which produce pearls, the 'children' of the magical shells, and those shimmering symbols of purity, the pearls that are found in the oyster, which would have been familiar from the earliest times to the makers of 'kitchen middens'.

The earliest conception of a deity as the personification of the female principle and power of reproduction arose from these beliefs connected with the cowry. They spread, so far as we know, from the area of the Red Sea to the eastern Mediterranean and were carried by migrating peoples to almost every part of the world reached by humans. Age-long beliefs in a 'god-in-the-shell' and legends of the birth of a woman or a female child from a shell, the goddess from the sea, are worldwide, as also are stories of creation having originated from shells.

The first idea of a Mother Goddess was probably of a deity born from a cowry shell. She was a sea-goddess, worshipped in sea-caves

63

Above Beliefs in the magical properties of shells are associated with the apertures of cowries and the shapes of other shells such as the ear shells. Key: 1 Egg Shell (*Ovula ovum*) 2 Map Cowry (*Cypraea mappa*) 3 Tiger Cowry (*Cypraea tigris*) 4 Lynx Cowry (*Cypraea lynx*) 5 Ass's Ear Shell (*Haliotis asinina*) 6 *Haliotis varia* 7 *Cypraea miliaris* 8 Money Cowry (*Cypraea moneta*) 9 *Calpurnus verrucosus*. *Right* The two cowries commonly used as currency; top: Gold-ringed Cowry (*Cypraea annulus*), bottom: Money Cowry (*Cypraea moneta*), both about 1 inch long.

and grottoes decorated with shells. Her voice was heard through the shell trumpets which summoned the people to worship and whose booming sound, like that of a muted fog-horn, carried further than any instrument then known.

In the Middle East, long before the rise of Greece, she was Ishtar; she was Ashtaroth who rose from Chaos and danced on the sea. In Crete, her palace sanctuary at Knossos, destroyed by earthquakes in about 1400 BC was carpeted with sea-shells. A triton shell was found in her early sanctuary at Phaestos and a carved gem from the Idean Cave shows a female figure blowing a shell trumpet before the sacred horns of the altar. As Aphrodite, goddess of fertility and love, she was born, according to the most ancient myth, of the froth of the sea *within* a shell which carried her to her island home on Cyprus and to which she gave her name, Cypraea, Giver of Life.

A polychrome bowl, classic Mayan style (300–900 AD) showing the Old Earth God seated in a conch shell.

On the other side of the world, in the New Hebrides, there is still a belief that the first woman came from a cowry shell. Certain tribes of north-west America believed that the first human was a female child born of the mating between a raven and a cockle, while ancient Mayan and Aztec pictographs frequently depict a tiny person emerging from a sea-snail, or human forms combined with shells.

Another legend from the South Pacific which closely echoes that of the birth of Venus as well as the American Indian legend mentioned above, comes from the island of Malekula. Here, the first woman came into being by magical influences in the shell of a Giant Clam (*Tridacna gigas*) which lay on the reef. Inside the shell she lit the first fire and a bird from the island, seeing the smoke, came and pecked at the hinge of the shell to open it. As the shell opened, the woman came out. Their son became the first chief of the island.

An echo of the same theme may occasionally be found in Christian churches. One of the misereres of Manchester Cathedral, for example, has a carving under the tip-up seat depicting a female child emerging from a conch shell and in the act of thrusting a spear down the throat of a horned and writhing dragon. Here, the angel or spirit of the shell is symbolic of purity conquering sin. A whelk (*Buccinum*) with a figure rising out of it was sculptured on the font of St Clement's church at Sandwich in Kent.

Perhaps the most remarkable manifestation of the cult of the cowry is to be found in America. The Money Cowry (*Cypraea moneta*) is alien to the whole American continent. It occurs only from the east coast of Africa and the Indian Ocean to the seas of the Pacific between Japan and the Great Barrier Reef, yet it has for untold centuries been one of the most sacred and revered possessions of American Indian tribes. Even the memory of it is enshrined in tribal legend. Its ritual uses and the beliefs associated with them bear an extraordinary resemblance to those which, in ancient times, were current in the Old World.

The tradition in America is that the original sacred shell, whose name meant 'symbolical of life', was brought by a hero-god who acted as intermediary between the Indians and the Great Unknown and who founded their Medicine Society. For ritual use, other small white shells might be used but the rare Money Cowry, handed down from generation to generation, was regarded with special veneration as being like that first brought to them by the god. Mystical powers are attributed to these shells and it is remarkable how closely the ideas of the American Indian about the connection of the Money Cowry with resurrection and rescusitation are linked with ancient beliefs as far afield as Europe,

African carvings of Eshu the go-between (on the right) and a messenger between man and the gods (on the left) wearing cowrie shell strings by which Eshu can read the future.

the Middle East, Africa and China, especially in ceremonies connected with death and burial.

The Omaha Indians possessed a sacred shell, of such antiquity that its origin was unknown. Handed down from generation to generation it was kept in a skin lodge concealed from sight within a package of mats and plaited skins. It was consulted as an oracle and taken on hunts to bring fortune to the hunters. Tobacco was consecrated by having been hung from the shell-package before being smoked at the Great Medicine of the tribe. At other ceremonies, magical cowries 'swallowed' by the medicine man were believed to pass their power to his medicine bag when he breathed upon it. Among the Ojibwa and the Menomini, Money Cowries were for centuries used in the initiation ceremonies of their Grand Medicine Society.

When Columbus initiated his voyages of discovery at the end of the fifteenth century and brought the first modern Europeans to the American continent, it is more than likely that some of them carried with them Money Cowries from Africa or the Indian Ocean where they were already in use as currency. It is known that, at a much later date, the Hudson's Bay Company attempted, unsuccessfully, to introduce the Money Cowry as a medium of exchange. This attempt failed because the native peoples already had well-established shell currencies of their own, but it is reasonable to assume that the Money Cowries held in reverence in certain Indian lodges had been acquired from the European conquerors and traders.

Beliefs in the magical powers of shells once widespread throughout both the Old World and the New and current to this day among many primitive societies from Africa and Asia to the myriad islands of Oceania, illustrate perhaps better than any other medium, the essential common origin and culture of the whole human race. The vital factor about shell magic is that it is usually *good* magic, benevolent, *white* magic, aiding mankind in his struggle against the unknown.

In east Africa, cowries were offered to twins. If one died, a 'double' was made for it and supplied with these life-giving shells. In Polynesia, shells of the Chambered Nautilus (*Nautilus pompilius*) are hung from the roof to keep away evil influences, while in the Dyak longhouses of Borneo, a mother will give her child the large, disc-shaped shells of a land snail (*Hemiplecta brookei*) to play with, or she will hang

66

them from a thong near his sleeping place, for these shells, known as 'moon droppings' are full of protective magic against evil spirits.

For many centuries, shipbuilders from Arabia to the Far East and Oceania strung protective cowries and other shells from the prows of their ships, believing in their strengthening powers as well as in the direction-finding magic of their 'eyes'. The Solomon Islanders of today string 'Egg' shells to the high stem of their sea-going canoes in exactly the same way and for just the same reason.

The Aztecs specially associated the snail shell with pregnancy, and so do the Japanese, to whom the cowry is the 'Easy Delivery Shell', held in their hands by women at childbirth to ensure certain and successful delivery. Indian and West African peoples have similar customs.

Belief in the magical power of cowries as 'givers of life' led naturally, according to the primitive train of reasoning, to belief in their power to revitalize or reanimate the dead. For this reason, it became the custom in many different parts of the world to put cowries and other shells into the grave or into the mouth of the corpse to ensure the continued existence and eventual resurrection of the deceased. According to ancient Chinese writings, nine cowry shells were placed in the mouth of a dead emperor, the Son of Heaven; seven in the mouth of a great nobleman; five in the mouth of a high official; three in that of an

uth of a common man.

ious result when cowries also came to
fore had two distinct properties, as
The practice of placing cowries, and
d them, as money in the mouths of the
Europe, these shells or
r ferrying the deceased

Ceremonial dancer from the Cameroons wearing mask covered with whelk shells. His coat is decorated with cowries.

Above Fetish mask from Mali, made of wood and decorated with cowry shells, 28 inches high.
Right A display of native masks, most of which have cowry shell eyes and are decorated with shell discs.

Cowry shells, shaped pieces of Mother-of-pearl Shell and sometimes the operculi of turbo shells are often used for making the eyes of tribal images, effigies and totems where their use is, no doubt, at the same time magical, artistic and appropriate. The Dyaks of Borneo, in their headhunting days, put white cowries into the eye sockets of the skulls which they hung from the rafters of their longhouses and which they believed brought strengthening additions to the vital essence and collective soul-substance of the tribe.

Even that humble mollusc the slug has its place in folklore as a harbinger of good luck. In the northern counties of England, for example, it used to be believed that if you saw a black slug in your path on leaving the house, picked it up by the horns and threw it over your left shoulder, the journey on which you were setting out would be prosperous. Thrown over the right shoulder it would draw down bad luck. In areas where belief in magic still persists, slugs, snails and powdered shells have their part in making spells and reading omens, in making charms and love-potions.

The best known shell in the mythologies of ancient Greece and Rome was the scallop shell in which Venus-Aphrodite, goddess of beauty and desire, was first brought from her birthplace in the sea. To the Greeks she was a daughter of Zeus, father of the gods. Some said that she was born of his union with the sea-nymph Dione; others that her origin was much earlier, almost at the beginning of the world, and that she was born of sea-foam impregnated with the semen of Uranus when his son Cronus, creator of the Greek nation, defeated him in battle and cast his genitals into the sea. Howsoever she was conceived, all agree that she rose naked from the waves and was carried to the shore in a shell. She first set foot on the island of Cythera but later she crossed the sea to Cyprus, accompanied not only by her terrestrial familiars, the sparrows and the doves, but also by dolphins which played around her and by sea-gods and tritons who rose from the depths to make music for her on their horns of shell. On Cyprus she made her home at Paphos at the western end of the island.

The booming of the shell trumpet to which he gave his name announced the rising of Triton from his home in the sea-depths. Ovid describes how, when the whole world was inundated by a great flood, Poseidon the sea-god called his son Triton and ordered him to blow on his shell trumpet the signal for the seas and rivers to retreat. He describes how Triton's sea-blue head, all encrusted with barnacles, rose from the waves; how he took his trumpet, a spiral shell twisted at the mouthpiece and flaring wide at the other end and blew a long, strong blast whose sound went forth from the middle of the sea to the edges of the world. Coins of Sicily minted before 400 BC show him holding his shell trumpet with both hands and blowing into it.

All the sea-gods and tritons carried shell trumpets. Mermaids and sea-nymphs came up to sit among the rocks on lonely shores and comb their streaming tresses with the long spines of murex shells. When the one-eyed giant Cyclops fell in love with one of them, the sea-nymph Galataea, he sang to her 'Oh Galataea . . . smoother than shells polished by the rolling waves', begging her to raise her bright head from the blue sea and not to scorn him though he was so ugly and uncouth.

The most famous shell story of the ancient world is that of Daedalus and the riddle of the spiral shell.

Daedalus, a member of the royal house of Athens, was also an initiate of the mystic cult of iron-smiths and an inventor, during what was then the Early Iron Age of Greece. It was said that he had been taught his art by the goddess Athene herself. Having killed his best apprentice in a fit of jealous rage he fled to Crete where King Minos welcomed him as much for his skills as for his royal Greek connections. However, his hot temper soon led him into trouble again. He fell into disfavour with the king and escaped with Icarus, his son, using the famous feathered wings.

King Minos, enraged at losing the unique services of the great master-smith, set out in search of him. He took with him a large triton shell and wherever he went he offered a rich reward to anyone who could pass a linen thread through the spiral of the shell from one end to the other. He well knew that this was the sort of problem which Daedalus, if he heard of it, would be unable to resist. And sure enough, when he arrived at Camicus in Sicily and Cocalus the king undertook to have the shell threaded, it was Daedalus who came forward with the solution. First he bored a tiny hole at the apex of the shell. Then he tied a thread of gossamer to the leg of an ant and put it into the hole. Around the wide aperture at the other end of the shell he smeared honey whose sweet smell lured the ant on and on round the spirals. When the ant appeared at the aperture and he could secure the gossamer thread, Daedalus then attached a linen thread to it and drew that through too. The legend does not tell us whether the ant got its reward as well.

The origins of the sagas of ancient Ireland are lost in the mists of antiquity. Parts of them were handed down orally among country families in Ireland and the Scottish Highlands at least until the eighteenth century when the first written versions began to appear. Many of them are the stories of Gaelic warrior-kings and heroes attributed to the legendary warrior-bard Ossian and relating to events and adventures of the third century and earlier. From them it is clear that shells were greatly revered and used on many ceremonial occasions. There are references to 'Halls of Shells' and to a 'King of Shells' or 'Chief of Shells' sometimes described as Ossian's father who, in other legends, is said to be the great Fingal himself. It is thought that the halls of shells which feature in the sagas may have been shell-decorated caves or natural grottoes similar to those so used and decorated in the Mediterranean in still earlier times.

The Gaelic heroes of Ossian's day feasted and drank from shells. Magical drinking horns are referred to and accounts of ceremonies in which 'the feast is spread . . . the shells resound . . .' suggest that shell trumpets were also in use.

Legends describing the creation and formation of that 'child of the shell', the pearl, are to be found all over the world and they bear a remarkable similarity.

Pliny describes how the pearl is formed by dewdrops falling into the opened shell of the oyster and being fertilized by the rays of the sun. The quality of the pearl thus formed, he says, varies according to the quality of the dew and the state of the weather at the time it fell. Pearls formed in cloudy weather are pale and lustreless. Pearls formed during storms are small and poor because lightning startles the oysters and makes them close too soon. Thunder too will ruin the conception of a pearl, resulting in one that is hollow and useless. A large, clear dew-drop, falling during fine weather, is the one which will form a really beautiful pearl.

The Roman author Claudius Aelianus however, writing in the second century AD, had an exactly opposite theory: according to him, it was the lightning flashing upon the opened shells which created pearls. Pearls were conceived during stormy weather and later, when the weather is fine and the sea smooth, the shells which are the mothers of the pearls can be collected and the pearls taken from their bodies.

An ancient Hindu belief, identical with the Greek, was that pearls were formed by dewdrops which fell into the shells when they rose to the surface of the sea in the breeding month of May. The dewdrops were converted into pearls by the action of the sun's rays. When Columbus first set foot on the islands of the New World in the Gulf of Mexico 2 000 or more years later he found the native people fishing for pearl oysters and their women adorned with strings of lustrous pearls. These people had an exactly parallel story to account for their presence. The pearls, they told him, were formed from petrified dewdrops impregnated by the heat of the sun's rays.

Legends of Babylonia, Egypt, India and China all include stories of the Dragon Kings, the Nagas, whose palaces, rich with treasure of pearls, gold and gems, lie at the bottom of the sea. Mythologies abound with dragons guarding pearls, the chief treasure of the ancient world, with pearls secreted under the dragon's tongue or hidden in the heads of sacred snakes and elephants.

Along the sea coasts of northern Borneo and in parts of the Sulu sea there is still a curious belief that some pearls are able to increase their size or even to multiply themselves. This belief, which is of very ancient origin, is that virgin pearls (those which have not been pierced) of fine quality, if sealed into a box or jar with a little natural rice, will either grow larger or will produce new, small pearls. Many women keep these 'pearl breeding boxes' and have shown them to the author, pointing out the 'improved' pearls and the 'new' ones. As the pearls grow, they say, so does the rice diminish.

Four Peruvians, three of whom are blowing shell trumpets.

The special reverence with which the shell trumpet has been regarded throughout man's history probably stemmed, in its origin, from the cult of the cowry. As religions developed, the trumpet made from a large shell became one of the most important instruments in the rituals of temple worship and in tribal ceremonies. They were first used in Crete during the brilliant Minoan civilization of the second millenium BC and played a vital part in all religious festivals. From that time their religious uses spread throughout the world to almost every part inhabited by man with the possible exception of Australia.

Their most important function, that of summoning the deity was part of the ritual in such widely separated places as ancient Mexico, Malaya, India, Central Asia, Indonesia, Oceania and throughout Europe from the Iberian peninsula to the Caucasus. They are used today by the Shinto priests of sea-girt Japan and in the Buddhist temples of land-locked Tibet a thousand miles from the nearest coast, while to millions of Hindus, the Sacred Chank Shell (*Turbinella pyrum*) is a holy object, indispensable as trumpet or libation vessel on every occasion of prayer or worship.

They have been used by primitive peoples for many centuries at marriage and funeral ceremonies, at the rituals of initiation and circumcision and especially at festivals connected with ploughing and the harvest. They are closely associated with the cults of sun-worship which link together the ancient religion of Crete with those of Indonesia to the east and America to the west, and with beliefs which, among early cultures, have been virtually worldwide.

Until quite modern times, a shell horn was sounded in the churches of Piedmont and Genoa during the services of Holy Week.

It is in India, however, that the ritual use of the Sacred Chank Shell and the cult of its sanctity have developed far beyond those of any other religion.

'Glory to thee, sacred shell, born in the sea and formerly held by Vishnu in his hand', says a Brahman prayer. The first incarnation of the god was undertaken in order to destroy the demon chank Shankhasura and regain the sacred Vedas which he had stolen and taken to his lair at the bottom of the sea. The defeated chank became one of Vishnu's

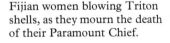

Fijian women blowing Triton shells, as they mourn the death of their Paramount Chief.

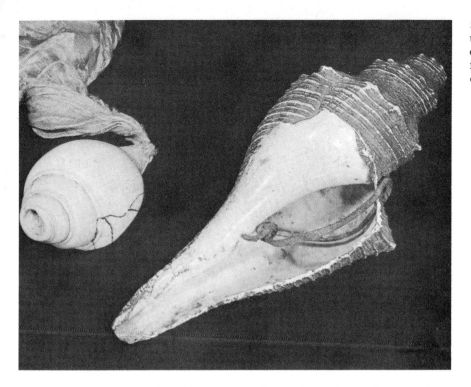

Shells used in Buddhist temples, in conjunction with other musical instruments, for accompanying religious ceremonies.

most important symbols and he is usually depicted in his human form holding the shell in his hand. The shell that he holds is a sinistral one.

Almost all spiral marine shells, when viewed from the apex, turn clockwise towards the right. Very rarely a reversed specimen appears, one whose whorls spiral anti-clockwise to the left. Such a shell, found only once among a million ordinary shells, is regarded with extraordinary veneration, as a holy relic, bringing blessings and good fortune to the fisherman who found it. It is destined to become the treasured possession of a temple. Mounted in silver or gold, delicately chased and embossed, it is the perfect emblem of purity and most fitting of all offerings at the shrine of the god.

Chank shells are used for making libations, for water poured from the mouth of the shell is holy water, used to bathe the images of the gods. A chank shell trumpet is sounded whenever the god Krishna is carried in procession. It is also used, in various parts of the subcontinent, at harvest rites and at weddings when it announces the tying of the marriage badge around the neck of the bride; as a libation vessel it pours holy water over the joined hands of the bride and groom. It is sounded at funerals and sometimes a shell is buried with a corpse. Among the Tamils, a chank may be buried beneath the first-laid stone of a new house to ensure good fortune and avert evil influences. In country areas a shell may be hung from the neck of a cow-buffalo in milk, a pack pony or a specially prized sheep, to protect them from being 'overlooked'.

For Christians, the use of shells is, with one remarkable exception, of small importance. There are a few valves of the Giant Clam brought from tropical seas on the other side of the world and presented to churches as novel and unusual baptismal fonts and holy water stoups. Such a one was the large specimen thirty-six inches across which was presented in the sixteenth century to Francis I of France by the Republic of Venice and which was installed as a font in the church of St Sulpice in Paris. Scallop shells have long been used in the baptismal service for the ritual pouring of water over the child's head. The conveniently shaped little scoop and shell-shaped dishes copied from it in silver, silver-gilt or wood were commonly known as 'scallops' and were often included in fifteenth-century lists of church ornaments, described as 'baptismal shells'. In later centuries, valves of the beautiful American Angel-wing Shell (*Cyrtopleura costata*) became sought after for the same purpose.

The Church, indeed, does not regard molluscs at all kindly. They figure among the 'unclean foods' forbidden to the Children of Israel by Jehovah. The eating of snails was sometimes permitted by special dispensation during Lent but they were also liable, among other garden pests, to be put under the ban of the Church. One can imagine the priest arriving at the vineyard with bell, book and candle, to deliver the following tenth-century exorcism:

'O ye Caterpillars, Worms, Beetles . . . Ants, Lice, Bugs . . . Snails, Earwigs and all other creatures that cling to and wither the fruit of the grape . . . I charge you by the many-eyed Cherubim and by the six-winged Seraphim . . . hurt not the vines . . . nor the fruit of the trees and the vegetables of (name of the owner of the land), servant of the Lord, but depart into the wild mountain, into the unfruitful woods, in which God hath given you your daily food.'

The outstanding exception, the only shell which holds a special and unique place in the Christian mind is the scallop-shell badge of pilgrimage and emblem of St James the Apostle, patron saint of pilgrims. Many legends comprise the story of the establishment of his shrine at Santiago de Compostela in the north-west corner of Spain, where the bones of the saint are believed to lie.

After the death of the Apostle, beheaded by the order of Herod Agrippa, his body was recovered by his disciples and carried away by sea. After a series of miraculous adventures they arrived on the coast of Portugal. Sailing northward they passed a village where a wedding had just been celebrated. The bridegroom and his friends were galloping on the sands when the bridegroom's horse bolted into the sea carrying him under the waves. Man and horse reappeared close to the ship and were saved by the saint's intervention. When they emerged from the sea, both horse and rider were festooned with scallop shells. The whole bridal party was baptized before the sacred ship sailed on, and took the scallop shell as the insignia of their saint. Further north, near the head of the Ria de Arosa in Galicia, the bones of the saint were laid to rest.

During the eighth century much of Spain was overrun by Moorish invaders and during those confused times the site of the grave was forgotten. But a hundred years later Theodorus, bishop of Iria, was said to have been led by a star to a cave where the sacred relics lay hidden. Others say that it was a humble peasant who made the discovery, guided to the spot by a supernatural light in the forest.

Near this place, which came to be called Compostela a shrine was built which grew, during the Age of Faith, to be one of the great centres of Christian pilgrimage. From the twelfth century when, at the end of the Third Crusade the Holy Sepulchre in Jerusalem fell once more into Muslim hands and Christians no longer had free access to the Holy Land, the Shrine of St James became one of the great pilgrim centres.

Early pilgrims returning home took with them scallop shells from near the shrine as tokens that their pilgrimage had been completed – and quite suddenly and spontaneously it seems, the great cult of the Pilgrim Scallop had begun. A scallop shell attached to the wide brim

Statue of St Roche, showing the pilgrim scallop badges on his shoulders. Made in the Joseph Fauchier Factory, Marseilles, France in 1725.

A view of Santiago de Compostela in Galicia, Spain.

of his hat, to his satchel or to his staff, became the accepted badge of the pilgrim. Many believed that the shell itself, emblem of the saint, would be a protection against the Devil and his fiends.

At Compostela, booths selling scallop shells, replicas and relics had begun to cluster around the new cathedral as soon as building began in the eleventh century. By the Middle Ages catering for the pilgrim had become the major industry of the town and the archbishops of Santiago were allowed special powers of excommunication against anyone found selling scallop shells outside the boundaries of the town.

Compostela had become, after Jerusalem and Rome, the third greatest centre of pilgrimage in the Christian world. The scallop shell emblem, at first associated only with St James, became the accepted badge of the pilgrim everywhere. It was even noted a century ago as far afield as Japan, worn on the sleeves of pilgrims climbing the holy heights of Fujiyama.

Hundreds of thousands of people visit Compostela every year. They buy scallop emblems in every size, form and material, from a valve of the natural object bought for a copper or two, to a perfect replica in solid gold or an enormous marble one complete with fountain jet, to set up in the garden.

Shells as Currency

Few people in western societies, beset by inflations, devaluations and fluctuating money values, realize that there still exist minor currencies based on certain shells, one of which has been in use for 4,000 years and which was, in its heyday, the most widely used currency the world has ever known. It was devised by man's ingenuity to suit his needs and eventually destroyed by man's rapacity. This is the shell currency based on two species of small, glossy cowries averaging about an inch in length. They carried with them into their new role something of their ancient aura of protective magic, of life-giving and luck-bringing.

The idea of money is thought to have arisen from the ritual of present-giving which is a feature of many primitive societies. From the first simple giving, elaborate systems of gift-exchange developed. Valuable objects had to be accumulated, for gift-making as well as for status and prestige, and cowry shells were among man's most treasured possessions. Gifts offered could not be refused and a gift of at least equivalent value but preferably of higher value must be offered in return. Many a man has been bankrupted by his obligation to make return, with interest, for gifts unwillingly received. Many another has been for ever disgraced by being unable to do so. 'Beware of the Greeks when they come bearing gifts' runs an ancient saying. This is usually taken to be a warning against their duplicity and treachery but it is more likely to refer to the fact that the Greeks will be expecting far better gifts in return.

The desirability of cowries as gift objects, as offerings for bridal and burial ceremonies, led to their being accumulated in very large quantities so as to increase the power of their magic. From these stores developed their use in barter, a simple exchange of possessions considered equivalent in value which still suffices for small trading over half the inhabited globe. Cowries, as a medium of exchange, were acceptable everywhere within certain trading areas and became a recognized form of currency. In other areas they remained objects of status and prestige or merely decorative ornaments – evidence of wealth but not regarded as money.

The perfect currency medium, the token which can be accepted as money, has yet to be discovered. Ideally, it should be something strong and lasting, difficult to break and more difficult to deface. It should be easy to handle, to count and to carry around, and above all it should be virtually impossible to counterfeit. Metals have answered most of these requirements better than any other substance with the remarkable exception of the little cowry shells. And these have one great advantage over metal coins in that they really are almost impossible to fake. They have been used as currency since long before man had discovered how to work metal and some of the very first 'coins' he ever made were metal replicas of a cowry shell. Those first metal coins, like the

Right 'Diwarra', one of the many shell currencies of New Britain threaded on to rotan strips and coiled into hoops 8 feet in diameter.
Below right Close-up of the shells showing backs broken off.

cowries themselves, were far easier to pick up or scoop up than the flat, disc-shaped coins which came later. Cowries are also decorative and beautiful to look at, smooth and pleasant to the hand and far cleaner than coins.

The two small cowries which form the basis of cowry currency are the Money Cowry (*Cypraea moneta*) and the Gold-ringed Cowry (*Cypraea annulus*). They are the most common of all cowries and are very easy to collect. They live in the warm shallow waters of the tropical and subtropical Indo-Pacific, usually under stones, coral and coral rubble close enough inshore to be exposed at low tide. In some places the ring cowries cluster in the rock crevices of the middle beach from which the sea recedes almost daily, when they can be scooped up by the handful.

One disadvantage of a currency based on these cowries is that they must all be single units of equal value. As their use spread and the vast quantities collected depreciated their initial value, enormous numbers were needed to complete large transactions. Other larger species such as the richly spotted cowry misnamed the Tiger (*Cypraea tigris*) have been introduced from time to time to represent larger denominations.

From early times cowries were known to western traders as 'porcelains' meaning 'little pigs', a name familiar to the thirteenth-century traveller Marco Polo who reported them to have been brought from India to the Yunnan Province of China. Their current name 'cowry' is adopted from the Hindu and Urdu names used in India.

The first people, so far as we know, to have used cowries as currency were the Chinese. Cowries have been found in Stone Age deposits as far inland as Shantung Province, and also replicas of them fashioned from bone, horn, Mother-of-pearl Shell and even stone. It is thought by some authorities that they may have been in use as long ago as 2 000 BC. Other specimens have been attributed to the tenth century BC and they were certainly in wide circulation throughout east China in the seventh century. Copies of them in copper and bronze were introduced during the sixth century and by the first century AD several species of larger cowries had been introduced as units of higher currency representing fixed numbers of the small ones. Sizes of these larger denominations quoted in ancient Chinese documents indicate that they could possibly have been the Turtle Cowry (*Cypraea testudinaria*), the Tiger Cowry (*C. tigris*), the Calf or Lynx Cowries (*C. vitellus*, *C. lynx*) or even the exceptionally large specimens of the Money Cowry which occur from time to time.

The cowry currency of China had a very chequered career. Due to the difficulty of finding a regular source of supply (later to become available from the sea of Formosa, the Philippines and the Sulu Sea), cowry currency was suppressed in 335 BC in favour of coins made from copper. It survived to be abolished again a century later. Two centuries later still, just at the beginning of the Christian era in the West, when the whole monetary system was riddled with debased coins and forgeries, the usurper-emperor Wand Mang abolished all metal coinage in favour of cowries and other shells and re-established cowry currency as the official currency of China.

As late as the fourteenth century, taxes in China were still being paid in cowries which retained a high value. In a good year a million or more would pour into the Imperial treasury. Although eventually superseded by coins, they were still in use until comparatively recently in out-of-the-way districts.

The career of the Money Cowry as a 'world currency' starts in the Indian Ocean hundreds, if not thousands of years later than its origin in China. Its centre was the Maldive Islands whose shell-collecting industry supplied the great distribution market in Bengal. The shells exported from the Maldives were the true Money Cowry (*C. moneta*). Arab writings of the ninth and tenth centuries describe how the wealthy and extravagant Queen of the Maldives, having used up her store of cowries to buy other treasures, would send her maidens into the sea with the long, fringed leaves of the coconut palm. These would be laid in the shallow water and the cowries would crawl on to them. Then the cowry-laden leaves were carried to the shore and the cowries shaken off to die and dry and be taken afterwards to replenish her inexhaustible treasury.

One of the earliest Indian references to cowry currency occurs in a Hindu treatise on mathematics written in the seventh century. It poses a problem in fractions combined with a sly dig at those who are mean in giving charity:

A beggar asking for alms was given

$\frac{1}{4}$ of $\frac{1}{16}$ of $\frac{1}{5}$ of $\frac{3}{4}$ of $\frac{2}{3}$ of $\frac{1}{2}$ of a dramma.

How many cowry shells did the miser give?

The cowry currency centred on Bengal was already well established when the Mohammedan invasion of the thirteenth century swept it along the trade routes of India. Its widespread use continued through 300 years of British rule when it became incorporated into the monetary system of the western rulers with a defined relationship to the rupee.

From India, their use spread west and north, into Afghanistan, through Persia and into Europe where they were known from the few magic cowries which had been carried there in prehistoric times along the amber-trading routes, and which have been unearthed as far away from their warm home seas as Vitebsk in White Russia where fifty were found in a Neolithic grave.

Arab traders carried the cowries across the Indian Ocean in their dhows, to be dispersed, at enormous profit, along the trading routes of northern Africa and down along the west coast. Up to a million of them could be bought in the Maldives for one dinar. By the time they reached Nigeria, one dinar would only buy 1 000. On the east coast of Africa, where the Gold-ringed Cowry (*C. annulus*) abounds, they were not so important, but when carried inland to areas remote from the sea, the Arab traders made sensational profits. When they first appeared in Uganda, for example, two cowries would buy a woman. Two generations later 2 500 of them would only buy a cow, about a quarter of a woman's price. So does the greed and enterprise of man kill his golden goose.

A seventeenth-century traveller in Bengal described the treasure houses built by kings and wealthy lords to store these shells which they valued as treasure along with their gold, silver and gems. He told of the Portuguese ships laden with rice from Cochin China, sailing to Bengal to exchange their cargo for cowries. Huge baskets containing about 12 000 shells, sold by weight, worked out at 9 000 or 10 000 to the rupee and could be expected to yield a profit of 200 to 300 per cent.

The dhows of the Arabs and the ships of the Portuguese were followed by those of the Dutch, the French and the English, trading mainly with the west coast of Africa and using the cowries to purchase slaves for the American market. As the riches of the East were opened up to western trade, billions of money cowries and a smaller supply of larger shells, poured into Africa.

Values varied greatly according to size, quality and the distance transported, whether by camel, donkey or human slave-porter. To be of value, the shells must be collected alive, their original high gloss intact. For larger transactions they would be strung in groups, sometimes with a built-in discount for cash. For small trading they were kept loose for easy counting. Dull, beach-worn shells were comparatively worthless. Enormous quantities were collected throughout the Indo-Pacific and a highly competitive and sometimes cut-throat trade developed throughout the various stages of their collection and distribution. It has been estimated that in the sixteenth century 100 million shells a year were being imported into West Africa alone. By the eighteenth century yearly imports had risen fourfold, to over 400 million. They were used mainly for the purchasing of negro slaves. Until 1807 when the British Parliament passed Wilberforce's historic bill for the abolition of the slave trade, British merchants were importing Money

Cowries from the East and exporting them to West Africa at the rate of some hundreds of tons per annum. Some even reached America, probably through the Hudson's Bay Company, but they did not become popular with the American Indian who already had other shell currencies of his own.

In India, cowry currency was used even in large transactions throughout Bengal, Hyderabad and many other parts of the subcontinent. One gentleman, for instance, paid over sixteen million of them for the cost of building his bungalow. This was at a time when their value was 4 000 to the rupee. The entire revenue of Silhet in Bengal Province was paid in cowries. At 5 000 to 6 000 to the rupee this amounted to some 1 500 million cowries every year in one district alone. No wonder that huge warehouses had to be built to store them and that a large fleet of boats was needed to transport them to Dacca, the capital.

In 1740 the value of cowry currency in Bengal was 2 400 to the rupee. A hundred years later it had fallen to 6 000 or more. The building of a church which cost £4 000 in the money of the day, was said to have been paid for entirely in cowries – over 300 million at the current rate of exchange.

By the middle of the nineteenth century, Hamburg merchants who had been importing money cowries from the Maldive Islands discovered that it would be far cheaper and therefore extremely profitable to load up with cowries closer to hand. These were the slightly larger but very closely related Gold Ringed Cowries (C. annulus) which could be collected in huge quantities on Africa's east coast and shipped from Zanzibar and Mozambique to the cowry-less west coast where a lucrative oil palm industry had succeeded the slave trade. The shipping companies vied with each other once again to seize the monopoly of this highly profitable trade. One Hamburg house alone sent fourteen ships annually to Zanzibar for cargoes of cowries. Records from the port of Lagos where a duty of one shilling per cwt was levied on cowries imported for trading, show that 65 496 cwts were imported in 1868; 56 040 cwts in 1869 and 50 340 in 1870.

Sometimes this trade resulted in Money Cowries turning up in very unexpected places as happened in 1873 when the British four-masted barque *Glendowra*, homeward bound from Manila with 600 bags of Money Cowries for the African market among her cargo, went aground in a thick fog and was wrecked on the rocky coast of Cumberland. For many years afterwards these little shells from tropical seas were rolled ashore by the chilly waves of the North Sea, to the great mystification of local conchologists.

This enormous flood of the little money shells inevitably depreciated their value. It now took from 60 000 to 100 000 to buy a young wife. In the Sudan, six or seven pounds weight of shells were worth only a shilling. On inland journeys, a slave would eat the value of his load of 20 000 shells in two to three weeks. The longest-lived and most widely distributed currency in the world's history was collapsing under its own weight, soon to become, as it had started, a small-change currency for the native market. Its value had fallen too low for it to be of any further use in trading on a wide scale.

Now that imports have dropped from a torrent to a trickle, it is said that the cowry is coming back into favour in certain parts of Africa and appreciating in value. It is still collected and strung on the coast of Somalia and sent to Zanzibar, from whence it makes its way via Aden to Addis Ababa and the remote parts of Ethiopia. In parts of Africa, the cowry is still the currency for small trading.

Up-country its value increases and over a vast area a buyer may even get better value for cowries than for coins.

Had their importation been controlled and the flood checked, cowries might well have continued as a useful minor currency to this day and cover an even wider area.

It has been suggested that in 1492, when Columbus set sail by an unknown route and discovered a new world, he or some of his men took with them cowry shells as trading currency. This would have been quite a sensible thing for them to have done, for cowries were known to be accepted currency in the 'Indies' which they hoped would be their destination. But if they did take any cowry money with them, they were soon to learn that it was unacceptable except as a curiosity or ornament, for the peoples of the strange islands they discovered and thought to be the 'Indies in the West', already had a highly specialized shell currency of their own.

The earliest reference to the shell currency of the American Indians known as wampum occurs in the *Voyages* of the famous French mariner and explorer Jacques Cartier. In an entry under the year 1535 he writes: 'The most precious article which they (the Hurons) possess in this world is the *esnoguy* which is as white as snow. They procure it from the shells in the river . . . of which they make a sort of bead which has the same use among them as gold and silver with us, for they consider it the most valuable article in the world. It has the virtue of stopping nosebleeding for we tried it.'

Wampum, the great shell currency of the American east coast, was but one among a number of shell currencies developed in America over many centuries before the advent of the white man. Its name is adopted from northerly dialects of the Algonquin language. Prehistoric trading routes have been traced along which shells for ornament and decoration and for use as money were passed from the coasts to inland communities. On Long Island, main distribution centre for the wampum of the east coast, shell mounds have been found consisting of a Venus clam (*Mercenaria mercenaria*) from which wampum was made, with the violet-blue or purple parts of the shell broken off. From these parts the more valuable wampum was produced. On the opposite coast, in ancient Mexico, the Aztecs paid a tribute in shells to their emperor Montezuma.

Wampum, however, was far more than a mere currency; it was an accountancy system which could be used not only for trading but for recording events. It was not only money but a substitute for writing, for mnemonic and symbolic purposes.

It was produced most laboriously by cutting or grinding small beads, usually about a quarter of an inch long and half as wide, out of certain shells, and then piercing the beads and threading them on to strings. The shell most commonly used was that of a common clam (*Mercenaria mercenaria*), known in America as the Northern Quahog and found all along the east coast from the Gulf of St Lawrence to Florida and along the Gulf Coast as far as Central America. It is an edible clam, commercially much in demand today for making chowder, the famous American stew or thick soup of which it is the prime ingredient. To the Indians it was not only food but wealth.

Other kinds of wampum were made from shells such as those of the Knobbed Whelk and the Perverse Whelk (*Busycon carica, B. contrarium*). In California a variety was made from the Purple Dwarf Olive (*Olivella biplicata*) and from oblong pieces of the highly coveted iridescent abalone (*Haliotis*). Button-shaped discs were cut from smooth clams very like the shell-string currency still used in Oceania. Very old strings of these clam discs, polished to an inimitable patina by many generations of constant handling, were especially highly valued. It is

Iroquois belt made of wampum.

thought that Francis Drake was referring to these when he spoke of the California Indians wearing 'Chains of Links . . . almost innumerable' and which he took to be made from pieces of bone. This was on th occasion, in 1579, when he reached his furthest point north in th Pacific on his great voyage round the world and had to take th *Golden Hind* into harbour on the coast of California for repairs.

By staining the wampum beads with various colours, by wearing the strings made into belts arranged in different combinations of these colours, the Indians were able to keep records, to send messages, to register events, transactions and treaties. White beads were used to denote peaceful happenings and happy occasions; purple beads recorded death, war and disaster. Each collection of belt records had its guardian or custodian, a tribal historian deeply versed in the language of the belt designs who could interpret the events recorded in the belts long after those who had made them were dead and forgotten.

Throughout the seventeenth and first half of the eighteenth centuries, the advent of white traders caused wampum to be in greater demand than ever. But when these white merchants introduced machines to mass-produce the little beads, the resulting inflation as the market was flooded ruined wampum as a currency forever. In the east it ceased to be used as money: in the north, the red blankets introduced by the Hudson's Bay Company were taking its place as a trading currency; in the west its use lingered for another century but its day was done.

On the east coast of northern America, 3 000 miles from the main distribution centre of wampum, another important shell currency had developed. This was based on tusk shells similar to those which had been among the most treasured possessions of Neolithic cultures in the Middle East 7 000 or 8 000 years ago. The species chiefly used was *Dentalium pretiosum*, a sturdy shell, solid and opaque, averaging two inches in length. It is shaped like a small, hollow tusk, slightly curved and tapering, of an ivory colour and sometimes marked with faint rings of dull buff.

These shells have been found in many ancient Indian graves in Canada and in the western and mid-western States. Those collected by the Haida nation of southern Alaska were the most highly prized; so much so, that although the shells could also be collected off California, the peoples there preferred to obtain their supplies from the far north.

It is probable that the shells from Alaska were believed to be imbued with the potent magic which has been associated with shells from the earliest human times and there is a legend that the tusk shells collected by the Haida had cost human lives. Not only that, but they had fed on man's flesh. They were slaves, captured in tribal raids. The killing was a ritual one. The slave was held face downward on a block of wood or stone and killed with a special stone adze known as 'slave killer'. His body was then weighted, lowered into deep water and left there for the carnivorous tusk shells to feed upon. After a certain length of time, the corpse was raised with a host of tusk shells clinging to its flesh, and it would be believed, as in other primitive cultures, that the shells had partaken of his essence, of his 'soul-substance'.

For currency purposes the shells were strung in fathom lengths (six feet). The value of a length was high, varying according to the size and quality of the shells. On average a length held forty shells and in the fur-trading regions would buy a fine beaver skin. But a fathom made

84

up of only thirty-nine shells was worth double; one of thirty-eight shells, treble.

Apart from their trading uses, *Dentalium* strings figured in an elaborate financial system covering payments for every occasion, from the smallest loss or injury to the price of a bride or the compensation for a killing.

Of the multitude of lesser shell currencies only a brief outline can be given here. In Africa there are many local currencies varying from iron and salt to beads and cloth but it is only shell money which generally is acceptable over wider areas. Glossy *Olivella* shells in the Congo; strings of snail shells; shell discs cut from the Great African Snail (*Achatina fulica*). Large cone-shell discs imported from the East Indies were once so highly valued that five of them would buy a tusk of ivory. The first natives who went from northern Rhodesia to work in the mines at Kimberley believed that the treasure for which the white newcomers were digging was not gold but the precious cone shells.

Throughout Oceania the variety of shell currencies is bewildering. Many are usually extremely localized. Values vary greatly from place to place so that a shell which has great purchasing power on one island may be a mere ornament on the next, a status symbol on a third, of value only for ceremonial payments on a fourth, and collected in large quantities on yet another solely for export. Some currencies have ceased to be used, some are now only used for ritual payments connected with marriage and death or the purchase of sacrificial pigs, while others have degenerated to symbols of wealth or personal ornament and are no longer used as currency. But many continue to flourish, and in Australia, New Zealand and Polynesia where shells have never developed into currencies, they have always been the principal trading objects, used in barter, in gift-exchange and hoarded as wealth.

Some of these shell currencies, the discs of shell pierced and strung together, are remarkably similar to the wampum currency of America. So are many of the beliefs and customs connected with them and with other shells, such as the right to wear certain armlets of shell beads according to rank, status or achievement, the patterns worked into them, their religious and magical qualities.

The making of shell money is a special craft, a mystique surrounded by ritual and magic, under such secrecy that those who use it know nothing of its origin or its making. Sometimes, special canoes belonging to the chief had to be used for collecting the shells. Some believe that the first shell money was made by gods or spirits long before the creation of man and certain very ancient shells, handed down through in-numerable generations, are to some islanders the most precious and revered of all, each one being individually known.

In Micronesia and Melanesia, over seventy different types of shell money have been identified. Most of them, however, fall into four main categories; the 'sapi-sapi' of the South Seas and New Guinea which is made of shell discs strung closely together like the beads of a necklace; 'pig money' which is made mainly of shell discs strung edge to edge on double threads; 'diwarra' or 'tambu' money made from the aperture and glossy outer lip of small nassa shells strung like beads; and the same shells strung flat or overlapping.

For making 'sapi sapi' of the common kind the clam *Chama pacifica* is used and the discs are white or whitish, but for the special strings of 'red money' which are much more valuable, discs cut from the less common thorny oysters (*Spondylus*) in red, orange or pinkish shades are used. In some areas these red strings are considered too precious to be used as money and are kept in the treasure-hoard of chiefs. In parts of New Guinea a man would pay a year's wages for one of these specials strings elaborately decorated with tassels and dangles.

'Pig money' is arranged in very complicated strings which, when completed, may reach fifteen yards in length and contain up to 20 000 separate discs. At the beginning is a fathom or so of assorted shells, a prelude to the pig money proper of shell discs set edge to edge in pairs or groups of parallel strings finished off with pigs' tails and separated by various charms and amulets. The very complicated uses of this strange money may never be completely known now that it is being so rapidly superseded by modern coin and paper currencies.

'Diwarra' or 'tambu' of New Britain is perhaps the strangest shell currency of all. In some communities it came to mean far more than money, it was a passion, an obsession, a cult, a way of life, its acquisition the be-all and end-all of existence. Nowhere else in the world has a money-form so shaped and dominated the lives of its inventors. A man's whole life would be spent in collecting it. No service however trivial might be given without payment; no present without return. Everything could be bought with it and everything had to be bought. Its chief value was for distribution after death and the more distributed the greater the honour and glory of the deceased. At the death of a wealthy man as much as 2 000 fathoms of pig money might be distributed, the only occasion when it was ever given away.

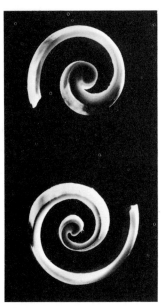

Transverse sections of the Blood-mouth Conch (*Strombus luhuanus* 2 inches long). Discs made from this shell were used as money.

To make this currency, small nassa shells (*Nassarius camelus*) were collected in huge numbers from the mangrove swamps around Bismarck Archipelago or purchased with the strings of the less valuable shell currency used in ordinary trading. The humped backs of the shells are then broken off, leaving only the aperture surrounded by the glossy, creamy outer lip. After bleaching, these pieces are forced on to strips of rotan, a task requiring considerable strength, each shell spaced evenly so as not to touch its neighbours, each length of rotan bearing up to 400 shells. The rotan lengths are spliced together in tens or hundreds and rolled into huge coils as big as cartwheels.

This extraordinary money is still so sought after as a symbol of prestige that even today its value is over two Australian dollars per fathom (almost ten times its 'official' value). Some pieces an inch or two long are still used for trading in the native markets but the longer lengths are too valuable to be used in trade. A huge ring of this money, eight feet in diameter and requiring four strong men to carry it, is valued today at A$3 000.

Of the many other shells used for making shell money in Oceania, just a few may be mentioned. Large cone shells and clams are cut into arm rings and used as money; so are pearl oysters cut into tongue-shaped or spade-shaped pieces and fishhooks made from the hinge part of the shell. The Egg Shell (*Ovula ovum*), banded forms of the common *Nerita polita*, bailer shells (*Melo*), olive shells (*Oliva*), the Geography Cone (*Conus geographus*), and cowries from the common Money Cowries to the rare and beautiful Golden Cowry (*Cypraea aurantium*), all have their adherents. And there are shell discs cut from many species including the small orange-red *Chrysostoma paradoxum*, the Blood-mouth Conch (*Strombus luhuanus*), pearl-lined bivalves of the genus *Isognomum*, the black pen shells (*Atrina*) and the common land snails. Of those no longer used as currency, many have reached the status of cherished family heirlooms and would not be parted with for any kind of modern currency.

Use and Ornament

There are very many ways, practical, ornamental, symbolic or emblematic, in which shells play their part in the human scene. Many of these uses are obsolete; some have declined, but others continue and new ones are invented as the ingenuity of man devises fresh ways of employing and enjoying these versatile creatures.

t as they are, lend themselves, by the very ctance, to a variety of practical uses. Such Great Scallop (*Pecten maximus*), the upper te and the lower concave like a little dish. tooth and non-absorbent, like porcelain. f an oven. The concave valve especially . So functional is their shape that similar lain or wood, came to be called 'scallops' dishes for butter, jam or sweets or other re often brought to the table baked in the hemselves are traditionally 'baked on the

mussels and smooth clams make excellent ghlands of Scotland, so Boswell tells us, of whisky. The shells of scallops and *Anodonta cygnea*) were used for skimming es of the Painter's Mussel (*Unio pictorum*) out Europe to hold their colours and by ous liquid of gold and silver used in their ansparent valves of the Windowpane Oyster for centuries used as a substitute for glass windows of very old houses in the Philippines. king beautiful lampshades and screens. (*Tridacna gigas*) and of species with smaller as splendid basins for fountains, for bird baths and flower containers.

The ancient Greeks used the valves of oyster shells for casting their votes at the elections. The voter scratched the name of his choice on the pearly-white interior of the valve, knowing that his mark could not be erased.

Another characteristic of the bivalve shell which has been put to ingenious use by man is the way in which the two parts of the shell fit together so perfectly at hinge and edge that no other valve will exactly match either. Together, they form a perfect little box or casket. Pliny tells us that the ladies of Rome prized such little shell boxes as containers for their cosmetics, especially when there were pearls still adhering to the valves. The Mayan peoples of Central America, whose brilliant culture reached its peak over 1 000 years ago, appear from

Procession during the Fiji
Hibiscus Festival at Suva
showing models of the Giant
Clam, cone and other shells
which live on the reefs of
islands in the group.

their remains to have used the shells of scallops and thorny oysters as
caskets to hold their most precious mosacis of iron and the sacred jade.
Victorian ladies used hairpin boxes, pinchushions and purses made from
bivalve shells.

In the west of Scotland there used to be a curious old custom which
put this characteristic of the bivalve shell to an unique purpose. When
two parties made a bargain or agreement, they would take a mussel, cockle
or oyster shell, separate the two valves and take one each. When the
transaction had been completed, one half would be handed over to the
holder of the other as a receipt. The united valves signified the termina-
tion of a satisfactory deal.

In eastern societies, the closely fitting edges of a small clam were
recognized as forming a useful pair of tweezers for pulling out facial
hair, long before a little metal gadget appeared on the scene.

The sharp edges of mussel, clam and oyster shells have also been used
by primitive peoples from time immemorial as knives, scrapers and
digging tools. Later societies ground and shaped them into fishhooks,
hoes, picks, hammers, gouges and a variety of useful implements
attached to handles of wood or bone with thongs of fibre or leather.

Almost all the larger univalves which complete their growth by
forming a wide, rounded final whorl, have suggested themselves to
man as convenient cups, pots, lamps, jars, buckets or scoops. The
largest of them all, the huge False Trumpet shell (*Syrinx aruanus*)
which commonly grows to twenty inches in length, makes a splendid
bucket. Triton's Trumpet (*Charonia tritonis*) can be used as a cooking

pot or kettle, its horny operculum forming a convenient lid and its canal a perfect spout. Helmet shells (*Cassis*), triton shells, frog shells (*Bursa*) and large whelks of all kinds have been used as lamps all over the world, usually suspended with the aperture upward to hold the oil and the wick laid along the canal.

The flaring apertures of bailer shells (*Melo* and *Cymbium*) make them especially useful, as their name suggests, for the quick bailing of small boats and canoes caught in tropical squalls. They are also used in native markets as scoops for sugar, flour and salt.

By the simple operation of breaking off the tip or boring a small hole near the pointed spire of a large univalve, a sonorous trumpet is made. In addition to religious and ritual uses these trumpets have been put to a host of practical purposes. The Greeks used them as war horns in fights on both land and sea; for calling assemblies of citizens and for setting the watch on the walls of their towns. In Japan, according to Pinto, the Portuguese traveller of the Middle Ages, shell trumpets were used as signal horns in war and also to warn of riot (one blast), fire (two blasts), robbery (three blasts) and treachery (four blasts). The name of the official shell-blower became the common word used to denote a braggart. Such trumpets have been used for centuries in many parts of Europe by herdsmen driving their cattle, by shepherds rounding up their flocks, by fishermen signalling to each other across wide stretches of water, and by watchers on lonely promontories to announce the approach of shoals. They have been used to send signals from village to village; to scare away birds from the crops; to summon labourers to their work.

In 1539 the Indians of Florida met de Soto's troops blowing conch shells and beating drums. In the West Indies, where a trumpet made from the Queen Conch (*Strombus gigas*) was used to call in the negroes labouring in the cane fields, the dinner interval between the blasts used to be known as 'shell blow'. In southern India and Ceylon

Bailer shell (*Melo amphora*).

The ridges of a cockle shell being used to make an indented pattern round the lip of a bowl.

A clay vessel in the form of a man blowing a conch shell, from Colima, Mexico. The conch shell was one of the insignia of the god Quetzalcoatl.

it was a trumpet made from the Sacred Chank which summoned the labourer to his work. In the south of France a shell trumpet was indispensable in making the 'charivari', that deafening serenade with which country people greeted the marriage of widows or 'ill-assorted couples'. During the Second World War, American servicemen stationed on lonely islands in the South Pacific heard the shell trumpet boom, maybe to call the native villagers to receive their dose of anti-malarial tablets. Shell trumpets still perform a useful function in many parts of the world.

Large, heavy shells have also been put to use as war clubs, as anchors for boats and sinkers for fishing nets. The Sacred Chank, because of its smoothness and weight, was used in India for polishing or glazing cloth, and in Nepal, so far from the sea, for giving a polished surface to paper.

In countries where land snails grow to a large size, their shells too are put to good use. The shells of great African snails (*Achatina*), often five to six inches long, make salt containers and are used as drinking cups, often to be seen floating on the water of the drinking jar. In Brazil, large snail shells were used as cups to catch the latex as it dripped from the rubber trees.

The substance of shells, being composed almost entirely of calcium carbonate, has led to yet another series of uses. Calcined shells make the finest and purest lime and this has been used in making a very fine glaze for pottery. A specially fine glaze for making an enamel for clock faces was obtained from cowries. In China, a lime made from ground cockle shells was mixed with oil to make the fine putty used for cementing coffins, for preparing surfaces for the frescoes and mosaics which ornament the gables of temples and the houses of the rich, and powdered shells were used to 'flock' wallpaper. In Bengal, lime calcined from the remains of the Sacred Chank shells cut up to make bangles used to be considered the very best and most auspicious for making whitewash for shrines and temples and for newly built houses, and in the countries of the East where betel is chewed, shells produce the fine lime which must be sprinkled on the betel leaf in which the areca nut is wrapped before chewing. Wealthy Malays use 'pearl lime', made by grinding and burning seed pearls from the Windowpane Oyster.

Calcined shells have also been used as dentifrice, and are given to poultry in their food to produce another kind of shell, as the internal shell of the cuttlefish, *Sepia*, (known as the cuttlefish bone) is given to cage birds. In areas such as Florida and Louisiana where large quantities of empty shells can be dredged, tons of crushed shells are used for road

The internal bone of the cuttlefish, *Sepia*.

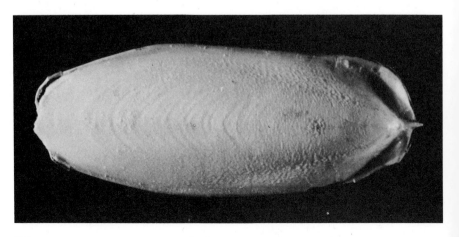

making, while crushed shells and coral bound with cement are made into building blocks.

Even the 'ink' of the cuttlefish has been used for writing and painting; it gave its name to the subtle dark brown tint known as sepia. Its powdered 'bone' was 'pounce', sprinkled on letters to dry the surplus ink.

The number of useful and beautiful objects made from shells or ornamented with shells by people of almost every culture throughout human history is legion. Those of the past can be seen in museums everywhere, in antique shops and salerooms; those of today in shops and stores particularly at coastal resorts and tourist centres and in the curio shops of the East. Polished turbo shells were long used as festive cups in Wales. The Green Snail shell (*Turbo marmoratus*) makes a superb drinking cup when the green outer layer has been partially ground away to reveal the light greenish and slightly iridescent pearl nacre beneath. These were polished and richly mounted in gold or silver set with jewels and used as goblets on ceremonial occasions. Such cups have been especially treasured among the royal families of Scandinavia.

Large shells of every description have been mounted as flower vases, or set on stands as objects of natural beauty, the Pearly Nautilus (*Nautilus pompilius*) being the most favoured for such treatment, especially when polished down to the rainbow-tinted nacre and delicately carved. Turbo and murex shells were mounted in silver and used as powder flasks; in China the paired valves of the Mother-of-pearl Shell (*Pinctada margaritifera*) are carved with designs of dragons, birds and flowers or with scenes from ancient legends and mounted on stands of blackwood. The Tiger Cowry has been made into saltcellars,

The valves of the Mother-of-pearl shell (*Pinctada margaritifera*) carved by Chinese craftsmen (contemporary).

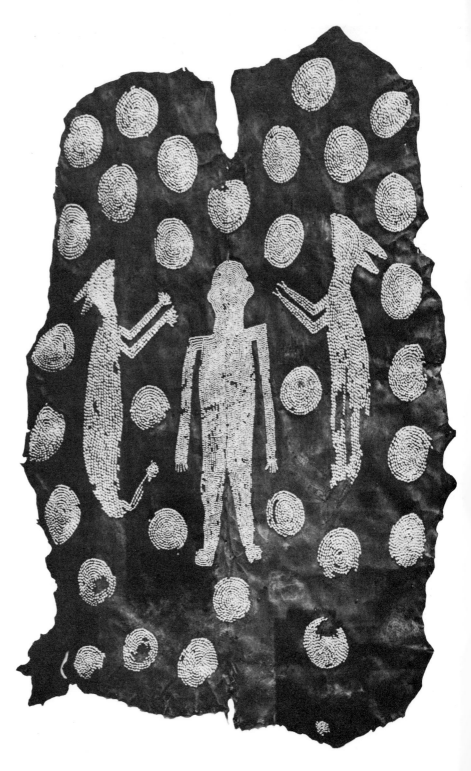

Deerskin said to have belonged to Powhatan, a south-eastern chief. The shell decoration is typical of North American Indian art.

ring stands, snuffboxes, ink holders, and mounted as soup spoons or ladles. Long, pointed shells such as the mitre shells (*Mitra*), auger shells (*Terebra*) and ceriths (*Cerethium*) have been made into pipes, while in India, small specimens of the Sacred Chank Shell have for many centuries been made into feeding cups for babies.

Victorian England 'went mad' about pearl shell. Virtually every man, woman and child in the land, apart from the poorest of the poor, wore a load of pearl buttons attached to every garment, from tiny ones no bigger than small peas to large discs elaborately carved and tinted.

Gloves, shoes and boots had pearl buttons, walking sticks and umbrellas had pearl handles; ladies carried reticules, card cases and purses made from pearl shell and wore pearl buckles on their belts. Gentlemen wore mother-of-pearl cufflinks, tiepins and fobs, carried coin cases and snuffboxes of the same material. In the home there were pearl spoons, letter openers, fruit knives and knife handles galore. In miladi's boudoir the manicure and sewing implements and their boxes, the pots and jars on her dressing table, her combs and brushes, pin-tray and hairpin box, were all likely to be made from or decorated with, mother-of-pearl.

For inlay work of every kind, Mother-of-pearl Shell has always been a favourite substance. It is hard; it can be cut precisely and polished to a rich sheen irradiated with every tint in the spectrum. Primitive peoples use it to make the eyes in their idols and totems and for decorating the carved prows of their canoes. For inlay work on furniture, on papier-mâché and lacquer articles, it is unsurpassed. It has been used for the decoration of crossbows, pistols, scabbards and sword-hilts, for the ceremonial trappings of horses and elephants and for beautifying a thousand articles too numerous to mention.

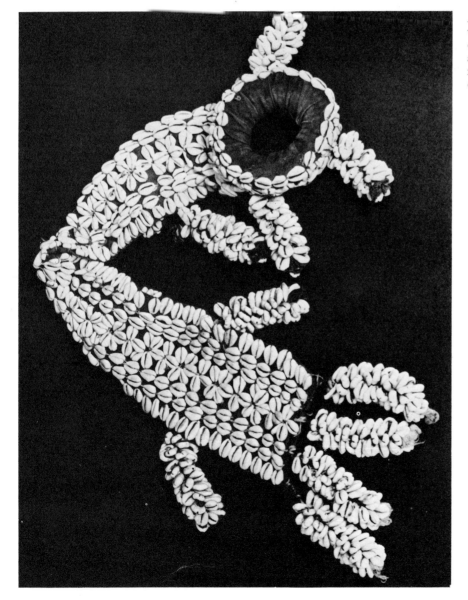

A padded head ring to balance water pots, decorated with cowries. The cowries were also supposed to provide magic protection for the carrier.

Many other shells are used for decorative purposes, from the cockle-shell edgings to garden beds and paths to the Money Cowries used in making mosaic pavements in the East and the avenue of orange and lemon trees whose trunks were inlaid with shells, described by visitors to Paramaribo in Surinam early in the nineteenth century.

For personal adornment, shells have surely been more widely used than any other product of nature. There can hardly be a woman or girl who has not, at some time, possessed a necklace or bracelet, a brooch, a ring or a pair of earrings made from shells. The modern woman who buys a set of shell costume jewellery at a beach resort, buys it only for adornment. Her more primitive sisters wear shells for adornment too, but also for belief in their other ancient attributes.

In Bengal, the bangles cut from the Sacred Chank Shell (*Turbinella pyrum*) are worn for religious and symbolic reasons, but they are also polished, carved and lacquered, ornamented with gold or set with jewels. Ornaments for headdresses, necklaces, long chains of coloured rings, buttons for coats and dresses, are all fashioned from the sacred shell, while finger rings are cut from lesser species.

In the longhouses of Borneo there are knee-length skirts completely sewn over with tiny mud snails (*Arcularia globosa*). Each shell has had the back laboriously ground off by rubbing on a smooth stone. Treasured heirlooms are long pendant earrings and necklaces strung from the same shells and of shell discs similar to the shell money of the South Seas, but used only as jewellery. These latter are said to be so old that their origin is unknown and there is no evidence that they were made locally. Similar strings of shell discs strung edge to edge in the manner of the 'pig money' of New Guinea, though never used as money, have been worn as ornaments by the native people of Chile.

The precious sandalwood from the New Hebrides, so highly esteemed in China, used to be paid for in a certain white, porcellaneous shell brought by sea-captains from the Tongan archipelago. The islanders of the New Hebrides so coveted this shell that they would exchange a ton of sandalwood for a single specimen. Yet they regarded it not as money, but as an ornament. Similarly, a tribe living in the central highlands of New Guinea (now Indonesian West Irian), so desired a certain form of the Money Cowry that their people would make tremendous journeys, crossing mountain ranges through passes 10 000 feet high, in order to obtain these shells from the lowlanders. They wanted only the very flat specimens, almost circular and ivory white, which occur occasionally among thousands of ordinary ones. These shells were their most treasured possessions.

In Tasmania, charming necklaces made from small iridescent Pearl Shells (*Elenchus irisodonta*) were highly prized as ornaments by the women of the now-extinct native people. Exactly similar necklaces are sold today in the curio shops of Port Arthur to tourists visiting the remains of the ancient convict settlement.

The convenient little Money Cowry, apart from its many uses as currency and ornament, has long been a favourite counter in playing games of chance. So have counters made from lozenges of mother-of-pearl. In China they were round, oval or oblong and ornamented with engravings and figures. To the avid card-players of Regency England they were 'fishes' and symbolized many a lost fortune or ruined life. In Wales, the passion for gambling involved even the humble snail. Rival snails were placed at the foot of a post. Bets were placed, goods and even small plots of land changed hands according to which snail reached the top of the post first.

Shell necklace from the Philippines made of dove shells.

For children shells have provided a variety of toys, from whistles and rattles to ingenious small animals. In the Orkney Islands children were still playing, within living memory, a shell game handed down for over 1000 years from the times when the islands were colonized by Viking communities from Norway. This was simply a game of 'playing farms', with stones and pebbles and bits of wood and shells picked up on the beach. When the farm buildings had been constructed and the fields marked out, shells took the part of the farm animals and the birds of the fields. The scallop shell, 'gimmer', was a sheep, its ribs and fluted corrugations resembling the fleece. The little cowry (*Trivia*) with its fine converging ridges, was seen as a little cat, 'cattiebuckie', a spired winkle as a dog and a variety with a longer spire was the sheep-dog, 'long neb'. The gaper (*Mya*) with its snout-like open end was 'grice', the pig, and the crow, 'kraa', was a mussel shell (*Mytilus*) with its long, blue-black, drooping 'wings'. The extraordinary thing about this game is that the Viking names used for these shells have survived a millennium virtually unchanged, since the links with Norway were broken. They are Norse names, still recognizable when compared with names currently used in northern Norway.

In Japan an amazing shell game was developed using no less than 720 clam-shell valves and based on the characteristic of bivalves already mentioned, that only the two valves of the same shell will match perfectly. Three hundred and fifty-eight of the valves could be paired and on the insides of each pair identical pictures or designs were painted. The remaining four valves did not match and had dissimilar designs inside. The valves were separated into two equal piles, each containing one of each matching pair. One pile was divided among the players, the other well mixed and spread out on the matting floor with the painted insides facing downwards. At a given signal these were turned over and the players matched up the shells they held with their other halves as quickly as they could. The first to do so was the winner.

Another and more difficult version of the game had verses inscribed inside one of the shell valves and a picture or design which could be coupled with the verse painted inside the other. These games were popular 300 years ago among the ladies of the Imperial Court and it conveys, in the matching of pairs, the idea that married people should suit one another and agree with one another as perfectly as the two halves of a clam. The four unpaired shells represented 'old maids' or 'ill-matched persons'.

Three sailor's valentines decorated with shells, which were popular souvenirs; made in the nineteenth century.

One of the most interesting aspects of the use of shells by man is their adoption as emblems or insignia, as symbols of rank, status or prestige. The use of a scallop shell as the badge of the Christian pilgrim has already been discussed but there are many other spheres in which a shell, or part of a shell takes on a symbolic value.

In Burma, a left-handed chank shell plated in gold and set with rubies formed part of the regalia of the king. The emperors of China invested their viceroys with a conch shell trumpet as part of their insignia. A sinistral or left-handed shell was credited with the power of being able to still the waves and calm the storms and was reserved for high officials whose duties took them on dangerous sea voyages. Such a one was the viceroy of Fukien Province who was also responsible for the administration of Formosa (Taiwan).

The Incas of the Andes pierced and stretched their ear lobes exactly as the Kayan people of Borneo do to this day. When stretched until the ear-loops hung to shoulder level huge ornaments of gold inlaid with figures of turquoise and coloured shell on a background of white shell, were inserted. These ornaments were the insignia of high rank. Among the Fijians the badge of high rank is much less of a burden – a rare and beautiful Golden Cowry (*Cypraea aurantium*). Among some of the tribes of Papua, a sugar-white *Calpurnus verrucosus* worn in the centre of the forehead is the insignia of a village elder.

Sepoy troops of the East India Company wore necklaces made from the canal of the Sacred Chank as part of their parade uniform. Hunting fraternities of the great Manding empire of Africa which reached its apogee in the fourteenth century in the area now covered by the Republic of Mali and neighbouring countries, wore elaborate headdresses decorated with horns and cowries and small hunting caps with rows of cowries set to resemble teeth. In Borneo, Dyak warriors of rank wore large polished valves of the Mother-of-pearl Shell (*Pinctada margaritifera*) nine or ten inches across, suspended from the fronts of their monkey-skin tabards. In Assam, a man who had killed another in war was entitled to wear three or four rows of cowry shells round the edge of his black kilt.

Perhaps the best-known and certainly the most easily recognizable status symbol of the western world is the coat of arms or armorial bearing and many of these display the device of a shell. Scallop shells have appeared in armorial bearings since the beginning of heraldry in the twelfth century and have continued to be used ever since. The scallop shell device added a prestige of its own for it implied connection with the great pilgrimages to Compostela, Rome or the Holy Land, and with the Crusades.

Early designs of the 'coquille' or 'escallop' showed two little holes like a pair of eyes pierced in the beak of the shell near the hinge. Such shells, which had been worn as pendants, were often found in ancient graves and the scallop shells worn by pilgrims must have been pierced so that they could be firmly sewn to the hat or satchel. The shell was almost always depicted with the hinge uppermost, the position in which it would usually have been seen fixed to the palmer's hat or hanging from his staff. Ancient beliefs in the magical propagation of oysters had extended to the scallop, for a sixteenth-century writer on armory described them as 'shellfish engendered of the air, and dew . . . the shell thereof is the fairest instrument that can be, being of Nature's making'.

A favoured design was to arrange five shells superimposed on a cross and this device, distinguished by a variety of colour combinations, was adopted by a number of families. An eighteenth-century poet explained their significance in the following lines:

The scallop shows a coat of arms,
That, of the bearer's line
Someone in former days hath been
To Santiago's shrine.

But some authorities on armory maintain that the scallop shell is borne not only as a badge of pilgrimage but by those who have held important naval commands or won great sea-victories or who have made long voyages. This seems very probable as shell devices continued to be adopted long after the days of pilgrimage had passed.

Other shells are occasionally used, the whelk, the cockle and even the snail. These are sometimes 'punning' devices alluding to the bearer's name such as the whelks appearing on the coat of arms of families called Shelley.

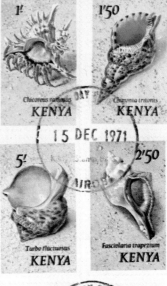

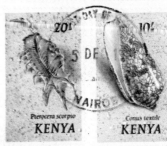

Kenya

DEFINITIVE ISSUE

OFFICIAL FIRST DAY COVER 15th DECEMBER 1971

ANGUILLA

10c TURBANS & STAR SHELLS

ANGUILLA

15c SPINY OYSTERS

3c STROMBUS SINUATUS
PAPUA & NEW GUINEA

CHARONIA TRITONIS
60c
PAPUA & NEW GUINEA

ANGUILLA

40c SCOTCH, ROYAL & SMOOTH SCOTCH BONNETS

ANGUILLA

50c TRITON TRUMPET

Turbo lajonkairii 1c
COCOS
(KEELING) ISLANDS

Tridacna crocea 2c
COCOS
(KEELING) ISLANDS

Tridacna derasa 3c
COCOS
(KEELING) ISLANDS

Coats of arms featuring shell devices.
Above left Sir Winston Churchill
Above right Arms devised for St James
Below left Shelley family
Below right John de Ufford

Shell emblems have also been adopted by societies, fraternities and orders of chivalry, such as the Order of the Ship and Scallop Shell founded by St Louis of France and conferred on members of the nobility who accompanied him on his pilgrimage to the Holy Land in 1248. The Knights of St Michael, an order created by Louis XI in 1469, wore gold or gilded collars of linked cockle shells from which a medallion of the saint was suspended. The badge of the Caballeros de Santiago, a Spanish religious and military order devoted to the protection of pilgrims on the bandit-infested roads to Compostela, bore the device of a red sword curiously shaped to form a cross, with a scallop shell on either side.

In the modern world the most widely known shell emblem must be the scallop shell trademark of the Shell Petroleum Company, familiar throughout the world on the flags of their tankers and at the petrol stations which sell their products. The brothers Marcus and Samuel, who founded the famous company, took the idea of the shell emblem from the original business started over a century ago by their father in a district near the Tower of London, then called 'Sailor's Town'. He used to buy the exotic oriental souvenirs brought home by sailors, especially shells from all over the world. At that time the sale of paraffin oil was merely a sideline. Until 1904 the emblem was a design based on the Sunray Tellin (*Tellina radiata*) but later the Pilgrim Scallop (*Pecten jacobaeus*) was registered as the official trademark of the company. Each of their many tankers is named after a different shell, a specimen of which is carried on board the ship mounted in a display cabinet.

Nowhere has a shell cult sprung up so quickly or flourished so exuberantly as the cult of the 'Pearlies', the costermongers of London's East End, who embellish their festive costumes with thousands of pearl-shell buttons. The Cockney costers have been a closely knit community from the Middle Ages, trading in the streets from donkey-carts and barrows or from stalls in the street markets, noted for their lively independence and quick repartee. Originally they sold apples (a large type called a 'costard' from which they took their name) but soon became the chief purveyors of fruit, vegetables, fish and shell-fish to the London poor. Leaders to act as spokesmen for the community and to organize protection against thieves and hooligans used to be elected by popular choice and became petty 'kings' of the costermonger fraternity. These positions tended to become hereditary and from them descended the Pearly Kings and Pearly Queens of today.

The origin of their passion for pearl buttons, which seems to have developed quite suddenly in the early 1880s, is obscure. But like many another sudden 'craze' it probably arose from a number of causes. There was the Cockney's natural love of finery. A well-to-do coster earlier in the century was described as wearing for his working clothes a waistcoat of broad, ribbed corduroy with fustian back and sleeves cut as long as a groom's coat and buttoned up nearly to the throat. Ornamental buttons also decorated the many pockets of this extra-ordinary garment, brass buttons with sporting designs being favoured with light-coloured corduroy and pearl buttons with darker colours. To complete the outfit he wore a small cloth cap tilted a little to one side, on which he could carry his baskets; and he grew his hair in ringlets at the temple.

Another impetus may well have come from the famous Cockney music hall star Albert Chevalier (1861–1923) who was the idol of the East Enders for many years. Chevalier appeared in one of his turns as a coster. To exaggerate his coster outfit he wore rows of pearl buttons down the jacket, the waistcoat, the sleeves and the sides of the trousers and on his cap, and his turn 'brought the house down'. There is also a possibility that some of the charitable, fund-raising activities in which the costermonger fraternity has always played a leading part, may also have had an influence. London's hospitals were at that time almost all 'voluntary', supported entirely by contributions from the community. They were always desperately short of money and many fund-raising activities had to be organized by their supporters. Costers and their families took part in processions, rallies and 'hospital days' and someone, whether coster or no, took part in one of them wearing a coat of eccentric cut and carrying a walking stick, both of which were completely covered with pearl buttons.

Whatever the cause or impetus, costermonger kings and queens in the various districts of the East End soon took to embellishing their holiday finery with pearl buttons, each coster king making up his own designs and vying with the others for the most splendid and eye-catching results. The 'tree of life' is a favourite motive, also hearts, ships, flags and flowers, stars, bells and geometrical shapes, even the coster's donkey with its cart, nothing comes amiss. The queens followed suit, crowning their costumes with regal hats lavishly wreathed with ostrich-feather plumes. And the little 'princes' and 'princesses' had to be dressed to match. As many as 60 000 buttons might be used on a single outfit, covering cap, jacket, waistcoat and trousers.

Above The Japanese shell
game set out with the box in
which the shells are kept.
The shells are clams (*Meretrix
meretrix*, about 3 inches long).

Left A close up of the clam and a matching pair of shells. The pictures have been painted on gilt paper, probably by the Tosa School of Artists at Kyoto, Japan.

Below A pair of Green Snail Shells (*Turbo marmoratus*, these specimens 7 inches long) ground and polished in Taiwan (contemporary).

Front and back view of a Pearly Queen, King and Prince. The costumes can contain over 60 000 buttons, sewn on by hand.

One of the sights of Edwardian London was the coster and his family setting out to enjoy a public holiday. The donkey cart, cleaned and polished after the week's work; a pair of dun donkeys with shiny brass trappings; the coster and his sons in their corduroys all agleam with pearl buttons; his wife and daughters wearing huge cartwheel hats trimmed with ostrich feathers dyed green, blue and red; all together filling the little cart to overflowing.

Such sights are seen no more. The destruction in the East End during the Second World War and the subsequent demolitions and re-building, scattered the costermonger communities for the first time. But the Pearlies have by no means disappeared from the scene. At least thirty kings and queens are still listed in the borough records. They turn out in all their glory for special gatherings, outings and festivals and they do splendid work for charities and good causes, proudly maintaining the traditions of their long history.

The Sacred Chank Shell of India, which was the national emblem of the State of Travancore, also appeared on its coinage until the end of its existence as a separate state at the end of last century. The

chank has also been represented on the coins of other ancient empires of India as the shell trumpet was used in the early coinage of Europe and the Middle East. Pre-Alexandrine coins of the fifth century BC bore designs of the triton shell, which also appeared on the coins of Tarentum around 400 BC and those of Byblus circa 350 BC. The earliest metal coins made in China were, as already mentioned, actual replicas of the Money Cowry. In the seventh century BC, the oval coins minted in the Greek colony at Lydia were also modelled in the form of a cowry. The little murex shell (*Murex brandaris*) which yielded the precious purple dye on which the Phoenicians founded their fortunes, was used almost constantly on their coinage from 112 AD onwards.

Two American States have officially adopted 'State Shells'; the Scotch Bonnet (*Phalium granulatum*) in North Carolina and the Horse Conch (*Pleuroploca gigantea*) in Florida. Many countries have issued beautiful stamps recording the glory of their shells. Those of Papua and New Guinea are richly coloured and clearly drawn; those of Kenya more delicately tinted and finely etched. Japan issued a special stamp commemorating a national shell show and featuring the rare Emperor Top Shell (*Pleurotomaria hirasei*). All pay tribute to the beauty of some of Nature's finest gems and record the appreciation of man.

Above Some of the types of shells most useful to man throughout the ages. Key: 1 Mother-of-pearl Shell (*Pinctada margaritifera*, this specimen 9 inches across) 2 Green Snail Shell (*Turbo mamaratus*) 3 Bailer shell (*Cymbium aethiopicum*) 4 Lamp shell (*Bursa bubo*) 5 Windowpane Oyster (*Placuna placenta*) 6 Tun shell (*Tonna sulcosa*) 7 Smooth Clam (*Meretrix meretrix*) 8 Great Scallop (*Pecten maximus*) 9 Mitre shell (*Mitra mitra*) 10 Swan Mussel (*Andonta cygnea*) 11 Marlinspikė (*Terebra maculata*).

Above right A spoon made from the Green Snail shell (*Turbo marmoratus*).
Right *Turbo marmoratus* polished and carved.

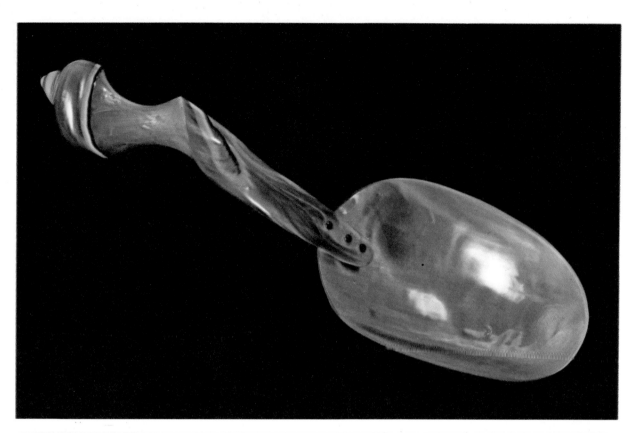

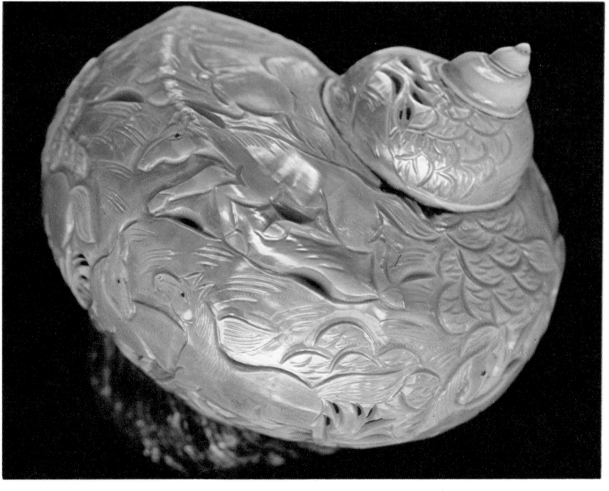

Commercial Products

In addition to the vast trade in currency cowries, the commerce in molluscs for food and their shells for many purposes, there are many other spheres in which the products of the mollusc have been exploited by man for his gain. They have provided him with some of the most beautiful and valuable of all his possessions.

Mother-of-pearl, the unique substance with which many molluscs line their shells is one of the loveliest materials known to man and it is as useful as it is beautiful. Its structure is of infinitesimally fine layers of pearly nacre each laid in microscopic grooves which break up light and reflect it in every subtle and delicate tint of the spectrum. It can be drilled, ground, treated with acids, engraved, sculpted, tinted and polished, yet the finest grinding and polishing will never level out those tiny built-in grooves and destroy their light-reflecting quality.

Its use is worldwide and as old as the age of man. Its uses are legion but it has probably never been used more extensively for a single purpose than in the making of pearl buttons, an industry which reached its peak in the late nineteenth century and has declined almost to extinction in the twentieth century with the advent of cheap, mass-produced plastic substitutes.

Pearl buttons were cut from many kinds of pearl-lined shells, but mainly from three species of large shells each of which produces a

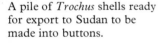

A pile of *Trochus* shells ready for export to Sudan to be made into buttons.

thick layer of pearly nacre. One of these is a bivalve, the Pearl Oyster (*Pinctada margaritifera*). The two valves are wide and shallow; some forms are large, up to ten inches in diameter, of a lustrous creamy white, faintly iridescent and sometimes with a golden rim. Other forms are silver-grey, moon-bright and dark-rimmed, known as 'black lips'. The other two are univalves: the largest of the top shells (*Trochus niloticus*), up to five inches high and thickly lined with rich creamy nacre; and the Green Snail shell (*Turbo marmoratus*), thick and rugged and formed, apart from its thin green exterior, of solid pearly nacre, with a very faintly greenish iridescence.

Mother-of-pearl buttons.

The manufacture of buttons from these shells is a long process which must be done by hand for no two shells are exactly alike and each button must be individually fashioned. From the univalve species, button discs are drilled along the spirals, large discs from the outer whorls, decreasing in size towards the spire. Each disc or 'blank' must then be shaped to the desired button form, incised, pierced for sewing, edges smoothed, bevelled, grooved or ridged and finally polished. All this just for plain buttons. Exquisite fancy buttons were made too, requiring the skill of highly-trained craftsmen.

Pearl buttons in various shapes, sizes and qualities were used on almost every garment worn by western man. They were manufactured by the billion, sustaining a substantial commerce which circled the globe. From the main fisheries in the tropical waters of the Indo-Pacific between the Sulu Archipelago and Australia, the Persian Gulf, the Red Sea and the Gulf of Panama, and from many lesser centres, pearl shell was collected by the ton and shipped to the main manufacturing centres of the world.

It was during the mid-Victorian era that the pearl shell trade, in England, for buttons and other articles, reached its height. By 1854, when the volume of trade had risen to a figure high enough to be included in the Ministry of Trade returns, 1 832 tons of shells were imported. In 1859 this had risen to 2 000 tons. France was importing similar quantities and large shipments were also going to Austria, China and to America to join the billions of Mississippi river clams already pouring into the button factories. Prices fluctuated so violently due to variable supply, demand and quality that, over a period of fifty years almost all prices between £60 and £600 per ton had been quoted.

Sheffield used a hundred tons a year for the manufacture of cutlery handles alone. Some 4 000 to 5 000 persons were employed in the trade in Birmingham where some firms were each turning out over seventy million buttons a year.

The shells arrived in bulk, unsorted, and a large proportion, especially of the larger ones which accounted for most of the weight, were damaged or worm-riddled and had to be discarded. There were many mounds of discarded shells in the Birmingham area; indeed it is said that the Town Hall is built on one of them. When prices were low, only the finest shells were used. When they went up, the discard mounds would be raked over in search of shells with useable parts. This accounts for the story of the altruistic workman who offered to clear up his neighbour's back yard free of charge – and made £20 from the discarded Mother-of-pearl Shells he carted away.

Shells of many other species were also imported but it is not possible to obtain accurate figures for these as most of them came in duty free as 'natural history specimens' and were not recorded. At the height of the nineteenth-century boom they included everything from rare and selected shells for the growing band of collectors to assorted

Above Suspended from rafts, cultured pearls mature in their oysters in the secluded waters of a Borneo lagoon.
Above right A Squid (*Sepiotuthis sepeioidea*) hovering in mid-water at night. A dye from the ink sac of the squid has been used all over the world.
Right The Noble Pen Shell (*Pinna nobilis*), the byssus of which was used in the manufacture of clothing.

shells in bulk to foster the craze for shellcraft, and beachworn shells collected along the tidelines and sold by the dealers as 'grotto shells'. The most common shells were bought up by street-sellers and hawked about the countryside for sale to village housewives and country children. Seven brokerage firms in the City of London advertised between them on a single day, October 10th 1871, a total of 1 059 cases of Mother-of-pearl Shell from Bombay, Egypt, Gambia, Panama, Fremantle and Manila; 637 sacks of cowries mainly from the Maldive Islands; 425 cases and thirty-nine tons of Japanese Ear Shells (*Haliotis asinina*); 22 000 Green Snail and other turbo shells; 1 400 helmet shells; 6 000 conch shells and innumerable bags, baskets and packages of assorted fancy shells. The conch shells were probably the Queen Conch (*Strombus gigas*) of which 300 000 were imported to Liverpool from the Bahamas in one year for use in the manufacture of fine porcelain.

Shells are still imported, mainly for the souvenir shops of holiday resorts, but never again on such a scale.

In India, during the same period, the chank shell bangle industry was also passing its peak. Bangles cut from the Sacred Chank have been worn by millions of women in India, Assam and Tibet for many centuries. In the extreme south, as ancient Tamil classics confirm, an important chank-cutting industry existed nearly 2 000 years ago. One of them tells of the men who dive for pearl oysters and chank shells and who know charms to keep the sharks away. Another ancient poem describes the chank-cutter's trade as it was in the second century AD, a description which would apply just as well today. The men sat on the ground holding the shell between the toes. Their legs were drawn up, the knees widely spread and pressed almost to the earth to keep clear of the great crescent-shaped, two-handled saw suspended from above which swung from side to side as it sliced through the shell. Boys had to be trained from an early age to accustom them to spending long hours of their working lives in this unnatural position.

The industry in the south was destroyed by the centuries of strife which followed the invasion and conquest by Muslim peoples from the north. Later it revived and flourished in Bengal which became the centre of manufacture. Calcutta became the main collecting centre for shells from the great chank fisheries of southern India and Ceylon. Dacca was the chief place of manufacture, from which the millions of bangles were distributed, mainly to women of the Bengali race, and exported to Assam and Tibet where there was a steady demand for the cheaper and plainer sorts. For the women of wealthy families there were bangles richly carved, jewelled, tinted and polished.

A survey made for the Government of Madras in 1910 showed that by that date, over-fishing had caused a severe decline in the numbers of shells collected. There was also a lessened demand from the wealthier ladies, who were developing a preference for gold bangles if their families could afford them, or glass bangles of European manufacture if they had to be content with something less expensive. These factors had caused the industry to diminish to an average of two and a half million shells per annum, over two thirds of which were imported from Ceylon. During the first half of the previous century, from four to five million shells were said to have been collected annually from the Gulf of Mannar alone.

A further consequence of the decline in chank shell fishing has been an even greater shortage of the rare sinistral specimens which are so deeply venerated (see page 73). During recent years, this shortage has led to the importation from America of the left-handed Lightning Whelk (*Busycon contrarium*) which is very common in West Florida. This is one of the very few naturally sinistral marine species and grows to sixteen inches in length. Large specimens of this species are now to be seen in many Hindu shrines and temples along with the true Sacred Chanks.

A cut specimen of the sinistral Lightning Whelk (*Buscyon contrarium*).

Another product of the mollusc, the manufacture of which became one of the greatest industries of antiquity but has declined in modern times almost to extinction, is the famous dye sometimes called 'Tyrian purple', the royal colour reserved for emperors and kings.

The complicated methods of extracing purple dyes from molluscs were known in the eastern Mediterranean and the ancient empires of the Middle East at least 5 000 years ago. They were still practised in many parts of Europe until quite recent times.

Crete is believed to be the place where the production of purple dye was first discovered and developed. The sea-faring Phoenicians became the chief collectors and distributors of this marvellous dye. They had arrived on the northern coast of Syria during the third millennium BC, founded the towns of Tyre and Sidon and become the first great trading nation of the early civilized world. They ventured as far as Spain and even reached the British Isles, mysterious Albion on the edge of the world, in search of tin. These cargoes they exchanged in Egypt for fine porcelain and glass. An Egyptian wall painting of the second millennium BC shows them clad in purple robes, bringing their merchandise to the city.

The first mention of the famous dye is found in a cuneiform text from Ugarit on the northern coast of Syria. Written about 1 400 BC, it lists a quantity of raw wool delivered to weavers who made the purple cloth. The purple-dyed cloth, when finished, was literally worth its weight in gold. There seems little doubt that it was the search for the murex shells from which the dye was extracted that became the driving impetus in leading the Phoenicians to found settlements all over the Mediterranean. Wherever these settlements existed, traces of ancient dye-works are usually found: huge mounds of the broken shells from which the dye-gland had been extracted; evidence of the rock-hewn vats on the sea shores where the dye liquid was prepared.

The Greeks ascribed the discovery of the dye to their hero-god Heracles who is identified with the Phoenician deity Melkart and with Baal. Heracles, according to the legend, was wandering on the sea-shore with his beloved, when her little dog picked up a shell as it was washed ashore and crunched it between his teeth. Later it was noticed that the dog's mouth was stained a marvellous purple colour. The lady exclaimed how dearly she would love to have a dress of just that glorious shade. Heracles, endowed with that enviable combination of physical strength and sharp wits which enabled him to perform twelve much more difficult labours, soon devised a way of collecting sufficient shell-juice to dye his lady a gown. The dye quickly became famous. It was used by Arachne who dyed her spun threads in all the colours made by the merchants of Tyre including the 'purple of the oyster'.

The Egyptians used it to dye the borders of their sails according to the rank of the captain of the ship. At the sea battle of Actium

Above A group of poisonous cones collected by the author in Sabah, North Borneo. The stings of some of them have proved fatal to man.
Key: 1 Literary Cone (*Conus litteratus*) 2 Textile Cone (*Conus textile*) 3 Geography Cone (*Conus geographus*) 4 Aulicus Cone (*Conus aulicus*) 5 Striated Cone (*Conus striatus*) 6 Imperial Cone (*Conus imperialis*) 7 Marble Cone (*Conus marmoreus*) 8 *Conus quercinus* 9 Beautiful Cone (*Conus pulicarius*) 10 *Conus catus* 11 *Conus sponsalis* 12 *Conus omaria* 13 *Conus lividus.*
Right Donkey's Ear shell (*Haliotis asinina*) was used in the Mother-of-pearl industry and was also supposed to have magical powers because of its resemblance in shape to the human ear.

in 31 BC when Octavius defeated Mark Anthony and Cleopatra, the ship of the Egyptian queen stood out from the rest of the fleet because its great sails were dyed with Tyrian purple. When Alexander conquered Darius of Persia in the fourth century BC, and took the city of Susa, he found there a treasure of purple cloth worth an emperor's ransom; 5 000 talents of it. Some of it had been stored for two centuries without losing its rich colour.

Moses used it in the furnishing of the Tabernacle and for the vestments of the High Priest. Roman senators were at first permitted a band of purple around the opening of the tunic, but in the first century AD, Nero decreed that the Tyrian dye should be worn by no-one but the emperor himself. Thus the dye came to be called the 'Imperial Purple'. Those who, becoming emperor, claimed the right to wear it, were spoken of as having been 'called to the purple'. Sumptuary laws apart, it was the exorbitant cost which prohibited its use by any but royalty and the extremely wealthy. In the reign of Augustus, because it took six pounds of the dye liquid to dye one pound of wool, the finished fabric vied in value with gold. During the more decadent days of the Empire, the dye was much in demand for making cosmetics to tint the lips and cheeks of Roman ladies.

After the fall of Rome its use declined. Murex shells, from which the dye was extracted, had been collected in such enormous numbers that they were becoming extinct in the eastern Mediterranean. The death-blow to the trade came with the capture of Tyre by the Muslims in 638 AD. After that the royal purple was used only occasionally for dyeing the robes of cardinals.

However, all over the world, the peoples who used shell trumpets also knew about the dye and how to extract it from various molluscs of the murex family. In northern Europe, centuries before the arrival of the Romans, purple dye was obtained from the common Dog Whelk (*Nucella lapillus*). The Venerable Bede, writing from his monastery cell in eighth-century Britain, described the dye extracted from a purple form of the Dog Whelk and used for staining parchment of vellum to set off the gold and silver lettering. It was of a lighter shade than the Tyrian purple. This dye was used thoughout the British Isles. Scottish and Irish crofters used it to dye their homespun tweeds. A visitor to a house in the west of Ireland in 1760, described the muslin gown worn by his hostess. It was 'flowered with the most beautiful violet colour' he said, and she told him that it was her own work and took him to the beach 'where she gathered some little shells . . . beating them open and extracting the liquor with the point of a clean pen, she marked some spots directly for me'. Deposits of broken Dog Whelk shells have been found in Connemara and Donegal, and also in Cornwall, and as this species is not suitable for either human food or bait, it is possible that they had been collected for their dye. The spires of the shells had been broken off (the usual method of reaching the gland containing the dye fluid), leaving the body whorl and aperture intact. One of these deposits, fifty-five yards long and from three to fifteen wide, indicates use over a very long period.

Mounds of the shells of dye-producing molluscs have been left by the ancient races of Japan; the method has long been known to the Chinese; and when the Spanish conquistadors arrived in Central America, they found that the natives there also used dye extracted from molluscs. The Indians of Mexico and Ecuador still use it, and they have devised a unique method of extracting the dye liquid without killing the mollusc. They 'milk' the living mollusc of its juice by

Two Dog Whelks (*Nucella lapillus*). This species was used for the extraction of purple dye.

gently squeezing and then replace it in its natural surroundings to manufacture more.

Many molluscs produce from certain glands a purple or violet liquid which is often strong enough to stain the insides of their shells in shades varying from pale mauve to deepest indigo. Many genera of the Muricidae – *Murex, Thais, Purpura, Coralliophila* contain purple colour. Sea-hares also exude dark, purplish liquid into the water around them when alarmed. The sepia dye of the squid, the deep indigo-coloured 'ink' of the cuttle have both been used the world over and used to be exported from China dried into little cakes for use as ink.

In the Mediterranean, it was two species of murex, *M. trunculus* and *M. brandaris*, which made the fortunes of the Phoenicians, and it was the long and laborious process needed to extract and prepare the dye which made it so costly. Pliny describes the catching of the 'purple fish' in osier baskets baited with cockles (exactly as whelks are caught to this day). According to Aristotle, the smaller shells of *Murex* and *Thais* were crushed and pounded whole because it was too difficult to remove the mollusc from its shell without damaging the gland containing the dye. The creatures had to be pounded up while still alive, for the molluscs exuded the purple liquid as they died.

The liquid is not, in fact, purple when first extracted; it is colourless and each mollusc yields only a few drops. But exposure to the light of the sun quickly turns it to a bright yellow which then turns to pale green and continues to change through bluish tints to purplish-red. These changes are said to take place faster or slower according to the intensity of the sunlight, factors of which the early dye-makers were well aware. More recent experiments with the dye of the Dog Whelk show

114

that its colour changes – from yellow through blue-green to indigo, blue, violet and finally a dull purplish-crimson – can take place in only a few minutes under direct sunlight but take several hours on a dull day.

The soft parts of larger molluscs and the crushed shells of smaller ones were thrown into open vats hollowed out of the rocks near the shore. Salt was added to prevent excessive decomposition of the flesh and the hot sun allowed to do its work for several days. Anyone who has collected live molluscs on the shore and failed to extract the animal immediately after death, can imagine the ghastly stench which must have polluted the air around these ancient dye-works. The next process was a continual simmering and skimming, adding water and slowly vapourizing it day and night over a period of ten days or until testing on strips of woollen cloth showed that the desired strength had been reached. It is possible that the great 'secret' of the Phoenicians was the discovery that the eggs of murex also contain the dye, and from them, of course, it could have been extracted far more easily. There is no evidence that they ever did so, but the fact that the dye liquid is also present in the eggs was accidentally discovered (or re-discovered) by Reaumur early in the eighteenth century when he was studying the eggs of the Dog Whelk.

What was it like, this precious purple colour of ancient kings? We do not really know, though various experiments have been made. There is little doubt that the master dyers of ancient times could produce a whole range of shades. By mixing the dyes from different species of molluscs, by adding nitre, urine, water, salt and seaweed, all the subtle tints from pale mauve to the dull crimson produced from the strongest concentration of the dye in *Murex brandaris*, could be manufactured. This dull crimson, a deep bluish-red with far more red in it than there is in the shade we think of as purple nowadays, was the most coveted and the most expensive; the noble and sacred colour of ancient kings and mediaeval cardinals. This shade was mainly produced at Tyre, while at Sidon, using *Murex trunculus*, a more bluish purple nearer to the modern idea of the colour was made.

Whatever the actual shades, these dyes were extraordinarily long-lasting. The purple borders of the robes draping a statue of Fortune dedicated by Servius Tullius for example, are known to have kept their colour for at least 560 years.

The exploitation of molluscan dye catered to a great luxury trade. In the Mediterranean there was also a small but exclusive trade in articles woven from the byssus threads of the Noble Pen Shell (*Pinna nobilis*) which the Romans called the 'silkworms of the sea'.

Many bivalve molluscs spin byssus threads by which they anchor themselves to rocks, corals or into sand. The threads are secrcted by a special gland in the animal's foot. Those of the Noble Pen Shell are of a rich and glistening, metallic, golden-bronze colour such as is seen on the backs of certain beetles, and so fine that they can be compared with hair, silk or spun glass. Each mollusc produced only a single gram of yarn. The spun yarn was woven into a 'cloth of gold' so delicate that a dress made from it for a Grecian queen could be pulled through a finger ring or a pair of gloves folded into a walnut shell. Yet it was so strong as to be virtually indestructible. Some like to believe that these byssus threads made the mysterious Golden Fleece which brought about the adventures of Jason and the voyage of the Argonauts.

On its own, or blended with a little silk, byssus cloth was made into shawls, scarves, cravats, gloves and stockings for the wealthy. The small industry centred around Taranto in southern Italy and the cloth was called Tarantine. Returning crusaders passing through Italy took articles of byssus cloth home to their ladies; in 1754 a pair of byssus-silk stockings packed in a tiny box no bigger than a snuff-box, was presented to the Pope. Articles made from it were shown at the London Exhibition of 1862 and at Paris in 1867, but the growth of the silk trade in Europe had already made it an anachronism.

The refulgent pearl, supreme jewel of the sea and one of nature's loveliest treasures, is the most highly prized of all the products of the mollusc. An unblemished pearl is one of the most ancient symbols of perfection, of beauty, of the purity of both mind and body. Yet it has aroused man's lust for possession, his greed and envy, his covetousness and his genius for destruction. It has inspired the poet – and cost lives.

The very doors of heaven are described as the 'Pearly Gates' and in the New Testament the kingdom of heaven is compared with a pearl of great price for which a merchant, once he had found it, went and sold all that he had to buy it. The vision of the New Jerusalem as revealed to St John was of an edifice with twelve doors, each of which was formed by a single pearl. Only wisdom is valued above pearls, but for a woman to be described as a 'pearl among women' is the highest praise of all and reflects the qualities of her character as well as the beauty of her face.

Pliny went even further when he spoke of pearls as the 'richest merchandise of all and the most sovereign commodity in the whole world'. In the Orient they have always been valued above any other jewel. It is said that, when the last empress dowager of China accepted a gift of diamonds from the new mines in South Africa, she thought little of them. Too hard, too cold, she said, unflattering to the skin and not to be compared with pearls.

In classical Rome, the trade in pearls was handled by a special corporation called the Margaritarii and only persons of certain high ranks were allowed to wear them. Julius Caesar gave a pearl worth 60 000 gold pieces to his mistress Servilia, but it is doubtful whether the lure of British pearls was really a factor, as Suetonius maintained, in his decision to invade England. Even so, he did send a shield studded with British pearls as an offering to the temple of Venus in Rome. During the days of the Empire, Caligula not only made his favourite horse a Consul, but gave it a collar of pearls into the bargain.

Long before the Roman era however, pearls had been among the most cherished possessions of man. In China, 4 000 years ago, pearls were among items officially acceptable in payment of tribute and taxes and listed a thousand years later as one of the products of the empire. They are referred to in ancient writings as having been known in India before 1 500 BC. Archaic Greeks and Etruscans were making jewellery bordered with pearls during the first millennium BC, and it is known that pearl fishing was being carried on in the Persian Gulf during the time of Alexander the Great (fourth century BC). In the New World, the Incas of Peru were so rich in pearls that quite humble people wore pearls worth a fortune according to their value in the societies of the West. Inca emperors wore sandals tied with strings of pearls and their ceremonial robes were pearl-embroidered.

116

Their pottery was decorated with scenes of pearl fishing, the divers going down from their reed boats carrying stones to weight them and nets in which to carry the pearl-oysters back to the surface.

In Europe, during the Middle Ages when both the rich and the not-so-rich carried a large part of their wealth upon their persons, pearls were worn in preference to all other gems in the extravagant jewellery to be seen around the courts of royalty. Renaissance jewellers suspended pearls from fine gold wires fashioned into airy earrings to swing before stiffened ruffs and collars of delicate lace. Strings and ropes of pearls were twined in the hair, coiled around the neck or draped over the shoulders. The large, misshapen pearls called 'baroque' were especially admired and accorded perfectly with their elaborate gold settings.

Kings wore pearls in their crowns; the Pope in his ring. Queens were expected to appear on ceremonial occasions wearing the world's finest pearls in size and beauty. Anne of Cleves, at the ceremony which preceded her brief spell as wife of Henry VIII, wore a wedding dress of 'rich cloth of gold embroidered with great flowers of large orient

117

pearls'. Mary Queen of Scots, previously Queen of France, owned a collection considered to be the finest in Europe. After she had been beheaded, Queen Elizabeth of England acquired this famous collection for about a third of its true value.

The pearl which was considered to be the most perfect and beautiful ever known was called the 'Pellegrina' and was housed at one time in the Zosima museum in Moscow. A perfect sphere weighing nearly twenty-eight carats*, it was so wonderfully brilliant that at first sight it appeared to be transparent. Other pearls which are ranked among the most famous jewels in the world are La Reine des Perles, weighing twenty-seven and a half carats, which was among the crown jewels of France until it was stolen in 1792 during the Terror; La Regente, an oval pearl of thirty-four carats which was also owned by the French Imperial Court; and, the most valuable in the world, the enormous baroque pearl, perfect in orient and colour, over two inches in length and four in circumference, owned by Henry Thomas Hope and known as the Hope Pearl. This fantastic jewel weighs 1 860 pearl grains (a pearl grain is equivalent to a quarter of a carat). The most famous of all American freshwater pearls, the Pink Queen, twenty-three and one quarter carats, was bought by Napoleon III's empress, Eugenie. In the Louvre, a magnificent necklace of 145 matched pearls weighing a total of 2 079 pearl grains, is estimated to be worth, at a rough estimate in the fluctuating values of the present time, some £250 000.

There are several instances of these lovely gems being wantonly destroyed to gratify an extravagant whim, such as the reputed occasion when Sir Thomas Gresham ground up a pearl for which he had paid £15 000 and drank it with a glass of wine to the Queen's health. She might well have preferred to have the pearl!

Pearls can be produced by very many different species of mollusc but those which are not made of the true pearly nacre have small value except as curiosities. The Queen Conch (*Strombus gigas*) yields occasional pearls of a lovely rose-pink tint, but they are not lustrous. Orange or yellow coloured pearls are sometimes found in helmet shells (*Cassis*), and very rarely an opal-white, pale pink or salmon-pink pearl may be found in the Sacred Chank.

Even the Giant Clam has its pearls, which appear like beads of dull alabaster or white porcelain. The largest pearl ever found came from one of these. Known as the 'Pearl of Allah', a huge lump weighing fourteen pounds, it was taken from a Giant Clam in the Sulu Sea in about 1920. The clam, according to local legend, is said to have trapped and killed the diver.

The pearl oysters were fished for everywhere they could be found; in Ceylon and the Gulf of Persia, in the Bay of Bengal, in Zanzibar and Mozambique, in the oriental fisheries of Japan, China and the Sulu Sea, in the South Pacific and Australia and in the Carribean and the Gulf of Mexico. They were fished for in the New World where Margarita Island (Pearl Island) in Venezuela yielded the lustrous rose-tinted pearls brought back to Spain by the conquistadors. Freshwater pearls from pearly river mussels were also collected. Those of Scotland, Wales, Bavaria and America were especially highly esteemed.

But the story of pearl-fishing is yet another chapter in the history of man's thoughtless greed. Overfishing and the appalling waste involved,

*The weights given are approximate as the value of the carat has changed over the years. It has now been set at one fifth of a gram.

118

were already destroying the industry before the discovery of pearl culture dealt the deathblow. Every oyster or mussel collected had to be killed and searched. Only one in thousands might produce a saleable pearl.

The freshwater pearls of the British Isles have been esteemed since before Roman times. They are found in the pearl mussels which live in swift-flowing rivers and mountain streams. Though usually small, their lustre is so fine and their translucent tints so delicate, ranging from white, through pink, every shade of green and brown to black, that they were often preferred to oriental varieties. Scottish pearls were in great demand in mediaeval Europe. In 1355 the jewellers of Paris were forbidden by statute to set them together with oriental pearls except in ecclesiastical jewels or church ornament. As is natural, the kings of Scotland owned some of the largest and finest. Until Stuart times the trade was considerable but by the mid-nineteenth century it had dwindled to a spare-time occupation for the crofters just before the corn harvest when work on the land was slack.

In 1967 however, the last of the full-time Scottish pearl fishermen found the most magnificent pearl yielded within living memory. He found the mussel in a backwater of the River Tay in Perthshire, lying below an accumulation of debris. Its treasure, known as the 'Abernethy Pearl' is half an inch in diameter, almost perfectly spherical and of exceptionally fine lustre and orient. Its basic colour is very faintly tinged with lilac. Such a pearl is unique for its match may never appear.

A pearl is said to be the result of 'an irritation in an oyster'. Though an over-simplification, this is basically true, for a pearl just does not happen naturally. The so-called 'natural' pearl is the result of disease, of deformity caused by overcrowding or the intrusion of some foreign body which the mollusc is unable to eject. Healthy, well-formed molluscs scarcely ever produce a pearl.

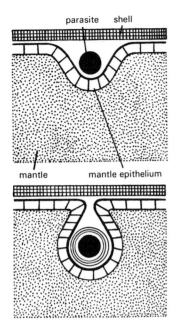

parasite shell

mantle mantle epithelium

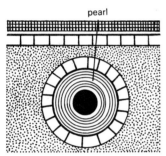

pearl

Above The stages in the formation of a pearl are shown from top to bottom.
Right An open oyster showing the cultured pearl inside which it has been grown over a period of three years.

The shell of the pearl oyster or mussel consists of three layers. The outermost is a thin skin of horny material called the periostacum. The central layer is of white and limey calcium carbonate. The inner layer, about ninety-five per cent calcium carbonate and five per cent protein, and of a different structure, is the nacreous layer which produces the pearl. Each of these layers is secreted by specialized groups of cells located mainly in the mantle which envelops most of the mollusc's soft body. It was not until 1913 that studies of pearl-bearing molluscs revealed that it is the pearl-building cells, torn from the mantle edges and carried into the flesh of the animal by intruding particles of sand, shell, marine worm's egg or other foreign body, that multiply around the intruder until they have covered it with pearl. This was the discovery which revolutionized the whole industry and introduced that marvel of the twentieth century, the cultured pearl.

The Chinese and the Japanese had known for many centuries that small objects could be inserted into a pearl-lined bivalve, between the animal and the shell, and would receive a coating of pearl. The discovery is said to have been made in the thirteenth century by Ye Jin-Yang, a Chinese of Hoochow. Small images of the Buddha in bronze or porcelain were put into freshwater mussels which were then returned to the water until the pearl layer had been formed. But only one side of the image, that adjacent to the animal, would be coated. The formation of a spherical pearl, coated all over with an even layer of pearl was a very different matter. That had to happen within the flesh of the animal; it happened naturally in only one mollusc in thousands.

The cultured pearl may truly be called the 'Jewel of Japan' for its development has been mainly achieved by Japanese industry and initiative. There is nothing artificial about a cultured pearl. Basically it is the same as a natural one, but the foreign body around which it forms has been introduced into the flesh of the mollusc deliberately and not by accident.

The story of the cultured pearl is almost synonymous with that of an extraordinary Japanese whose life story is a saga of perseverance, determination and the will to succeed crowned, after decades of failure, by such success as comes to very few. Kokichi Mikimoto was born only five years after the warships of Commodore Perry had forced open the gates of Japan to trade and contact with America and the West. He died in 1954 at the age of ninety-six having devoted most of his long life to realizing his dream: the cultured pearl. The eldest son of a humble noodle-maker, he was helping to support his family at the age of eleven. As a young man, he paid his first visit to Yokohama, the new port opened to foreign traders, and there he saw pearl shell and pearls and fell in love with them forever.

He started a business in marine produce and spent every spare moment studying pearls and the oysters which made them. Always concerned with quality, he was chosen to supply pearls to the empress dowager. He developed oyster 'farms' where young oysters could be sheltered and protected. He experimented with endless patience to discover how the accidental pearl might be made to happen on purpose. He suffered setback after setback; disaster upon disaster. But he never gave up and finally achieved his aim, proceeding to build up one of the most flourishing and successful enterprises of the century. The secret, well-kept at first, is now universally known: he placed the bead in the gonad gland of the oyster, and with it a tiny fragment of live tissue from another oyster, containing the pearl-producing cells.

His enterprise stimulated another dying industry. Freshwater mussels from the rivers of the American Middle West proved to be the most acceptable material for making the nucleus beads. These mussels had been so over-exploited for their pearls and for button-making during the past century, that they were in danger of extinction. Now, after a long period of rehabilitation and under modern ideas of management, the beds are yielding hundreds of tons of shells every year for shipment to Japan, to help make those sea-jewels which are now so reasonable in price that they are no longer the perquisites of queens.

Women separating cultured pearls from the debris of the oysters after they have been opened.

The Mollusc as Food for Man

When it comes to a question of survival, most molluscs are edible. Some, such as the oyster, provide the most delicate and delicious food the world has to offer; others are the source of coarser but still nourishing fare. The Swan Mussel (*Anodonta cygnea*), for example, which fattens in the muddy beds of ponds and lakes, few would eat by choice but in times of famine it has preserved thousands of poor families from starvation.

Molluscs both of land and shore were among man's first stable sources of protein food. Many have provided a double or even treble bounty, offering the uses of their shells and other products as well as the nourishment of their flesh. The flesh of the pearl oyster feeds the diver; the meat of the purple dye shells (*Murex brandaris, M. trunculus*) is eaten in the Mediterranean today as it was in Phoenician times, though the famous dye of antiquity is no longer extracted. The flesh of the Noble Pen Shell (*Pinna nobilis*) is still esteemed as it was by the Greeks when Plutarch, describing an Attic banquet wrote:

And pinnas sweet, and cockles fat there were
Which the wave breeds beneath its weedy bed.

though their shining byssus threads are no longer woven into cloth-of-gold. In America, the Northern Quahog (*Mercenaria mercenaria*), which provided the Indian nations with food as well as with shells for making wampum, is still relished for making chowders. The meat from hundreds of species whose shells adorn the cabinets of museums, shell dealers and collectors, has been eaten before the empty shells were sent to market.

Tastes in molluscan food vary tremendously, as they do regarding every other form of nourishment. In some countries, snails are relished; in others abhorred except by a tiny group of gourmets. In some, squid, cuttlefish and octopus appear on the menu daily while in others they are used only as bait for catching fish. People of one village may rate the flesh of a certain clam very highly; a few miles along the coast one is told that the same species is not fit to eat or that certain molluscs are not eaten except by widows and orphans (a mild form of charity practised in some Borneo fishing villages).

Of all molluscan foods, however, the oyster is certainly the king. The taste of oysters is the most delicate; they are as nutritious as milk and so easily digested that a very large quantity may be eaten without overloading the stomach, thus making them ideal 'starters' for a meal however simple or elaborate. An additional virtue to many has been their long-established reputation for possessing aphrodisiac qualities. In the opinion of many a connoisseur over the past 2000 years, they are best of all opened alive and swallowed whole, bathed in the sea water they hold within their shells. In the whole wide range of

An old Dutch drawing (1627) depicting an angel cooking oysters.

human foods there is nothing to compare with the experience of an oyster eaten in this manner. This was the way our earliest ancestors ate them and, despite the hundreds of recipes for cooking them which exist, many consider that the first and simplest way has never been bettered.

Of all the European species, the British native oyster was considered to be the finest of all. So highly were they esteemed by the epicures of the Roman Empire that British oysters were carried all the way to Italy and transplanted to artificial beds such as those on the Lucrine lake. After resting and fattening in their new quarters they appeared on the tables of such gourmets as Montanus who, according to Juvenal, 'could tell at the first bite whether an oyster had been bred at Circeii or on the Lucrine rocks'. He was but the forerunner of the nineteenth-century American oyster experts who knew, as they lifted an oyster from the pile, 'where it came from, how old it is, whether it is a Delaware, Prince's Bay or City Islander, or has grown under the dashing waves of Rockaway'.

Pliny the Younger, gently chiding a friend who had failed to turn up for a meal with him and had dined elsewhere, said, 'I had prepared, you must know, a lettuce and three snails apiece; with two eggs, barley water, some sweet wine and snow . . . but the oysters, chitterlings, sea urchins and Spanish dancers . . . were, it seems, more to your taste.'

With the advent of Christianity another problem was posed to the lovers of shellfish, not only of molluscs, but also of lobsters, crabs, crayfish and all other seafoods usually grouped under this name. For the edict of Jehovah, passed to the Children of Israel through Moses and Aaron, ruled out all these delicious foods as 'unclean': 'These

124

shall ye eat of all that are in the waters; whatsoever hath fins and scales in the waters, in the seas and in the rivers, them shall ye eat. And all that have not fins and scales in the seas, and in the rivers, of all that move in the waters and of any living thing which is in the waters, they shall be an abomination unto you.' (Lev 11:9).

Sometimes special dispensations were issued giving permission for shellfish to be eaten at certain times, but on the whole, the prohibition was ignored: such delicious food could not be allowed to go to waste. Besides, it was greatly needed by the growing populations and the time was to come when the succulent oyster would become the chief protein food of the urban poor in many countries.

Throughout the centuries the popularity of oysters never abated. Early in the thirteenth century, King John gave the fisheries of the famous 'Milton native', finest of all British oysters, to the Abbot of Faversham. These beds remained in the Abbey's possession and were a considerable source of revenue for over 300 years until the dissolution of the monasteries of England by King Henry VIII.

In the sixteenth century, foreigners visiting England were much impressed by the fine quality of the oysters hawked around the streets at a few pence the bushel (approximately four bucketsful). The waters of the river Thames were then so free from pollution that oysters could be kept alive for as long as twelve days by immersing them in the brackish water of the tidal reaches, and still be sold as 'fresh'.

Even in those distant times it was realized that on occasion the oyster needed a measure of protection against man. An Elizabethan law of 1577 for example, prohibited dredging in the oyster beds at the mouth of the Medway river between Easter and Lammas (August 1st, Feast of the First Fruits). During the Stuart era, numerous edicts from the Star Chamber prohibited the export of 'oyster faggots' (the fascines to which young oysters attached themselves), and the export of mature oysters when the price rose from eightpence per bushel to six shillings.

During the following century, oysters were still cheap and plentiful, a 'food for all', popular with the middle and upper classes as well as with the poor. Samuel Pepys could give his friends a New Year's breakfast of 'a barrel of oysters, a dish of neats' tongues, and a dish of anchovies, wine of all sorts and Northdown ale'. By the end of the century 200 could be bought for four shillings from the hucksters' barrows in London streets. According to Smollett, the clear green colour of the oysters from the coasts of Kent and Essex, prized above all others by the connoisseur, was counterfeited in London by keeping ordinary oysters for several days in 'slime pits' full of 'vitriolic scum'. The stomachs of Londoners in those days must have been as tolerant of toxic substances as are those of the resilient oysters.

It was the population explosion brought about by the growing momentum of the industrial revolution which spelled the doom of the English native oyster. Teeming millions in the urban areas needed ever larger quantities of cheap food; cheap bread; cheap protein food, cheaper than the meat of animals which was beyond the reach of the poor. Molluscan food was the answer; oysters, mussels, cockles, the harvest of the sea. This was the nourishing food so cheap that even the poorest could afford it. Thus began the rape of the oyster – and mussel – beds on an unprecedented scale, a scale which was soon to make a sour joke of the long-assumed belief that supplies of this cheap yet delicious food were inexhaustible.

By the beginning of the nineteenth century such huge quantities of oysters were being dredged and sold in the cities that they had become

An oyster seller of the nineteenth century, from a painting by H. Morland.

an essential part of the poor man's diet. As the inimitable Sam Weller remarked, 'poverty and oysters always seem to go together . . . the poorer a place is, the greater call there seems to be for oysters . . . here's an oyster stall to every half-dozen houses. The street's lined vith 'em. Blessed if I don't think that ven a man's wery poor, he rushes out of his lodgings and eats oysters in reg'lar desperation.' (Charles Dickens, *Pickwick Papers*, 1837). When Dickens wrote those lines, oysters still cost only fourpence a dozen. By the end of the century they had become so scarce that only the wealthy could afford to eat them. They have remained a luxury food ever since.

It was about the middle of the century that oysters quite suddenly became scarce and therefore expensive. Huge quantities were still being dredged from the depleted beds where the numbers of young correspondingly diminished. From one fishery alone, in the Whitstable area whose oysters had been famous from the time of Henry VIII, more than 50 000 bushels were sent to the London market in a single season. By 1865, their price had gone up to three halfpence each – extraordinarily high by the standards of the time. During the oyster seasons of the 1880s (from September to April), it is estimated that 800 million oysters were consumed in London alone and at least as many more in the rest of the country. Probably twice this huge quantity could have been sold if they had been available at a lower cost, for the price had rocketed to ten guineas a bushel. A Commission appointed by Parliament to investigate the fishing industry of Ireland, reported in 1864 that the great oyster beds of Wexford had scarcely any oysters in them.

Variations on this sad theme could be repeated in many parts of the world. In France in spite of royal decrees and government edicts, reckless dredging using iron-toothed dragnets and iron rakes continued unabated. In 1861 and 1862, oyster boats at Granville took over thirteen million oysters. The annual yield from the famous beds at Cancale in Brittany dropped from seventy million oysters a year in the 1840s to a miserable single million in the 1860s. 'Oyster wars' were fought between rival fleets and naval vessels called in to guard the beds from complete devastation, for it was by then realized that the depleted beds could not, as had been hoped, replenish themselves by 'spontaneous generation'.

In America, oysters in New York had once been so plentiful that they could not be sold. A sea-captain in the seventeenth century reported continuous oyster beds on the sea floor extending for at least fifty miles, from Rockland Lake on the Hudson River to Sandy Hook. The vast oyster beds in the area of the Chesapeake River covered some 3 000 acres and produced, in the 1880s about twenty-five million oysters a year. On occasions, over 100 000 bushels have been taken in a single day from this, the greatest oyster-bed in the world and long believed to be inexhaustible. A hundred and fifty special oysters boats, sailing from New York, handled millions of bushels per annum, and the famous Chesapeake Bay oysters were exported to both London and New York. Yet from the beginning of our own century, while the human population has risen from some seventy-six millions to nearly 200 millions, oyster production has declined from around 160 million pounds of oyster meat per annum to only fifty-five million pounds in 1965.

At long last, the unpalatable truth had to be faced. Oyster beds were not inexhaustible; neither, if over-collected, were they self-replenishing. The devastation which had gone on for so long unchecked could well result in the complete disappearance of the oyster from our shores. Even if we mended our ways and controlled the industry very strictly, the damage would take many years to repair.

Led by the French, who were well ahead of the rest of the world in the study of oyster culture and the breeding of oysters in well-protected artificial beds, attempts were made to retrieve the situation. A Fish and Oyster Culture Company was formed in England to set up 'oyster parks' similar to those already successfully established in France. One of the first such projects for preparing artificial beds was initiated by the South of England Oyster Company which proposed to operate off Hayling Island. Attempts were made to introduce species more hardy than the delicate English native. Portuguese oysters; French, Dutch and American; all have been tried with varying degrees of success.

Man had over-exploited once again, and was rapidly contaminating with his industrial and human wastes, just those sheltered estuaries

Crushing Slipper Limpets (*Crepidula fornicata*) on board a British Ministry research vessel.

where the depleted oyster population might best be re-established. But man is by no means the oyster's only enemy. There are the starfish, the boring sponges, the winkles and whelks which bore through their shells and suck out their luscious juices. In addition to these, the English oysters now have to contend with two new predators, introduced along with the American oysters tried out in their beds. These are the American Slipper Limpet (*Crepidula fornicata*) which sits in clumps on top of the oysters and suffocates them, and the American Oyster Drill (*Urosalpinx cinera*), both of which settled down and flourished mightily in British waters, though the American oysters with whom they came as uninvited guests found the water of the British Isles too chilly.

In the present century, other forces have taken their toll. Mysterious diseases further ravaged the beds during the 1920s. By the early 1960s, new methods of cultivation were bringing about a small if steady improvement and the damage and neglect of the war years had been repaired. Then disaster struck again. The exceptionally cold winter of 1962–63, when the sea off the east coast of England almost froze, virtually destroyed the native oyster. A few beds in the south-west escaped complete ruin, only to be damaged again five years later by severe oil pollution from the ill-fated tanker *Torrey Canyon*. Fortunately, in that year the east coast oysters began to breed again and the long-famed and once so plentiful English native escaped extinction once more.

In 1973 the wholesale price of oysters in London's Billingsgate market ranged from £5 to £10·50 per hundred.

Oysters of various kinds are eaten throughout the world wherever they occur, and so are mussels, particularly the widespread and prolific Edible Mussel (*Mytilus edulis*). Even more nutritious than oysters but not quite so easily digestible, they are usually eaten cooked. They are very adaptable and can live in huge colonies because each one takes up very little room and needs only a tiny space on some solid surface to which it can anchor itself by its byssus threads. If the threads should be torn loose, it can settle in another spot and spin some more.

Mussel beds actually play their part in helping to preserve our coastline from erosion, acting as barriers against the encroaching sea. In 1865, when beds of mussels extended for miles along the Norfolk coast, the lord of the manor of Heacham brought an action for trespass against the local inhabitants to prohibit them from taking mussels from the seashore. The great Norfolk beds helped to bind together and strengthen the embankments and jetties built along the coast to hold back the sea and prevent flooding. At Bideford in Devon, where surging tides continually washed away the mortar from between the stones of the town bridge, the spaces between the stones were filled with young mussels. These anchored themselves firmly into the cracks and provided a much more efficient plaster. Needless to say, by order of the town corporation, it was forbidden to collect these mussels!

The man credited with being the first ever to cultivate mussels was a thirteenth-century Irish sailor named Walton who was ship-wrecked on a deserted stretch of the French coast in 1235. He had the idea of making nets from woven sea-grass for catching the seabirds which skim along the surface of the water in search of food at dusk. He had to fix his nets to wooden stakes driven into the muddy bottom when the tide was out. History does not tell us whether he actually caught any birds. What he did catch on the incoming tide was a whole lot of mussel spawn which settled on the stakes and began to grow. He had accidentally discovered a much more reliable source of food. Giving up the net idea, he concentrated on making the first artificial mussel-bed. Two rows of stakes forming an angle with the apex pointing out to sea were driven into the mud at the level of the lowest tides. He then made the stakes into a rough fence by lacing them together with long branches and even fixed wicker baskets in the narrow gap at the

Below left Edible Mussels (*Mytilus edulis*) feeding underwater, showing frilly inhalent siphon and smooth-edged exhalent siphon. *Below* Clumps of Edible Mussels (*Mytilus edulis*).

Above Rednose Cockles (*Cardium aculaeatum*) stranded after a storm in Torbay, Devon, where they are collected for food.
Above right An Edible Cockle (*Cardium edule*) underwater, showing extended siphons.
Right Hydraulic cockle dredge trials in the Thames estuary.

point of the angle to prevent any trapped spawn which had not settled on the stakes from being carried back to sea. Similar methods are used in France to this day.

An acre of good mussel-bed can produce 10 000 pounds of meat in a year – 500 times as much as an acre of pasture land, which, during the same period, produces only 200 pounds of beef. In the future, cultivated mussels may well become a major source of protein food to help feed our hungry world. Yet millions of people in Britain have never tasted a mussel. Many have probably never even seen one, for about half the catch is used as bait and the rest goes mainly to the Midland counties where the mussel, both fresh and bottled, is still popular.

Bivalve molluscs are generally the most popular for human food. In addition to the oysters and the mussels, there are the scallops, cockles and clams. In times of scarcity ashore many a seaside community would have perished but for the cockle. It is so prolific that good beds can produce as many as a million and a half cockles per acre. Razor clams (*Solen*) were considered great delicacies by the Greeks and the Romans. In Japan they were so highly esteemed that an

ancient law forbade people to fish for them until sufficient had been
caught to supply the household of the emperor. Charles Kingsley
praised them as 'very good to eat' and pointed out that they 'abound in
millions upon all our sandy shores'. Pen Shells (*Pinna*) too, have been
esteemed from ancient times and praised as highly as the scallop for
flavour and delicacy.

Of the univalves, the most easily accessible and therefore most
commonly eaten are the limpets and abalones which cling to rocks
within easy reach; the winkles which can be collected in shallow
water among the stones and seaweeds at low tide; and the whelks which
can be caught in baited baskets rather like lobster pots. The abalone of
the Channel Islands and Brittany, locally known as the ormer, has often
been claimed to be the most nutritious of all seafoods: 'an epicure
would think his palate in paradise if he might always gourmandise on
such delicious ambrosia', enthused one connoisseur. Pacific species
of this family have always been great favourites with the Chinese and
it would be a poor feast which did not include some dish containing
slices of abalone.

Whelks, one of the seafoods considered good to eat at any time of

131

Spearing razor clams (*Ensis siliqua*) in Torquay, Devon. The spear has a small arrow-like head which is pushed down the hole into the clam.

the year, feature in the accounts of Canterbury Cathedral for 1504 when 8 000 of them were bought at five shillings per thousand to be served with sturgeon at the inaugural feast of a new Archbishop. Nowadays they would be unlikely to appear on any such similar occasion. The little winkle used to be consumed in enormous quantities in London. In 1861, 10 000 bushels were shipped from Belfast alone and it has been estimated that the total intake was around 2 000 *tons* per year.

In Britain, the once huge consumption of molluscan food has dwindled to a tiny trickle. Of forty species listed in Lovell's book on edible molluscs in 1867, only a very few are eaten today and none at all on a national scale. But on the Continent and in the Mediterranean, molluscan food is as popular and widely used as ever, the basis of many famous national dishes. Among the molluscs eaten are the land snails.

Snails are eaten in very many parts of the world and considered very pure food as they live only on the freshest green vegetation. They even enjoy a small place in history as having assisted the legions of Rome. When the great general Marius was besieging the castle of Jugurtha, set high upon a rocky eminence, it was one of his soldiers who, while collecting snails, accidentally found a way up to the summit. The best time to eat snails is just before cold weather sets in.

132

133

Garden snails (*Helix aspersa*) being fattened. They have been used as food since Roman times.

They have eaten their fill and are at their plumpest, ready to secrete the tough film (epiphragm) with which they seal up their apertures ready for the winter hibernation. In France they are not considered in season until late October or early November.

The snail garden of Fulvius Hirpinius, described by Pliny around 2 000 years ago, had separate sections for different species of snails, one of them being the Great African Snail (*Achatina fulica*) noted for its fecundity (as we know to our cost today). Hirpinius fed his snails on meal and new wine and fattened them for the market to enormous size. Another authority recommended that the snail garden should be surrounded by a ditch to hinder the escape of the snails. A ditch, he averred, would be much cheaper in the long run than having to keep a slave specially to catch the runaways. Shells of the Roman or Apple Snail (*Helix pomatia*) have been found by archaeologists on Roman sites in Britain. Some people have taken these as evidence that the Romans introduced the species to Britain, but they are more likely evidence of Roman partiality for the snails, which were probably established when they arrived, and possibly that the Romans built snail gardens on the Roman pattern. Snail gardens still flourish in many parts of Europe and the snails are fattened for the market much as they used to be in Roman times.

In France, several species are cultivated and they are also collected in the open country and from vineyards. The 'vineyard' snail which has fed on the vine, is esteemed above all others and has for long been exported to the United States for the delectation of American gourmets. The 'wild' ones are often starved for a while before eating in case they have fed on plants which might be harmful to humans. They used to be the staple meat of many poor country people who had no other meat all the year round except perhaps at Easter.

Snails have never been as popular in England as they have always been on the Continent, though they are still eaten around the ship-building areas of the north-east. Eaten with salt or vinegar they are

134

served as a tasty snack in public houses and working men's clubs.

The Great Snails of Africa, so popular with the Romans, are eaten in many parts of that Continent. They are said to be best at the end of the rainy season when the flesh is at its fattest. The large, round swamp snails (*Pila*) which live in rice fields, mangrove swamps and other moist, muddy areas, are an important protein food to many people in tropical lands. Some of the smaller species such as *Pila scutata* are said to compare favourably with the edible snails of Europe.

Millions of people in the world today live almost entirely on a diet of seafood. In many countries, molluscs feature among the most popular national dishes: the bouillabaisse of France, the paella of Spain, the chowders of America, the octopus of Greece, the stuffed squid of Italy, the everyday cuttlefish dishes of all Mediterranean countries and the endless variety of molluscan titbits served when drinking wine.

Many molluscs are eaten raw, simply sprinkled with a little lemon juice or vinegar. Many people prefer them in this, their simplest form. But there are hundreds of recipes for cooking them. The famous French dictionary of the kitchen, the *Larousse Gastronomique*, lists thirty-three recipes for cooking oysters; thirteen for mussels; twelve for clams and many more for winkles, cockles, snails, octopus, squid and cuttlefish. The Spanish cuisine could list as many more, and the sum total of European recipes could be doubled or trebled in the Orient.

The strangest method of cooking of all, however, must surely be the one described by the seventeenth-century diarist Evelyn who saw a 'fire-eater' performing his feats. He put a live coal on his tongue with an oyster upon it, 'the coal was blown on with bellows, till it flamed and sparkled in his mouth, and so remained till the oyster gaped, and was quite boil'd.'

The oyster barrow may have disappeared from London's streets, the barrow boys – and girls – no longer cry 'Cockles and mussels. Alive, alive, O!' but whelks and winkles, cockles and mussels may still be bought from stalls outside the pubs of the East End on a Saturday night. There are signs, too, that molluscs are coming back into favour. Frozen squid are appearing in some markets and the women's magazines are giving advice to housewives on how to cook them. The Northern Quahog or Hard-shelled Clam of America, which arrived in English waters, it is believed, on the hulls of ships and settled down very happily on the south coast, is now being harvested and put on the market together with instructions for making the traditional American chowders.

A word of warning must be added. There are dangers in eating shelled molluscs 'out of season', especially the bivalves which filter their nourishment from the water. The season for eating them fresh is during the cool months of the year, in England, from September till April. Even then, they should never be used if the shell is even slightly open. During the warm months when the sea is laden with planktonic algae on which they live, they gorge on microscopic organisms which are highly toxic to humans and which can cause a paralysis which may result in death. They have also learned to adapt to life in polluted waters which no human could tolerate, and to absorb poisons which could be fatal to our less resilient flesh. Outbreaks of cholera in southern Italy during 1973 were traced to mussels collected from polluted water and large areas of mussel-bed were subsequently destroyed by order of the authorities.

The Helpful and the Harmful

The seven seas of the world abound with stories of terrifying sea-monsters and sea-serpents which attack ships, overturn boats, drag sailors to their death and lie in wait in sea caverns to seize and drown the unwary diver. Such widespread tales and legends, however far-fetched and exaggerated, usually contain some small kernel of truth and most of the sea monsters and sea dragons can be related to the great cephalopods, the squid, the octopus and the cuttlefish.

In eastern legend it is the many-headed sea snakes and naga dragons which guard treasures and destroy the humans daring enough to approach their lairs. Tales from the pearl divers of India, the East Indies and Polynesia describe huge octopuses 'two fathoms broad over the centre and each arm nine fathoms long', which seized the fishermen's boats and dragged them down. Sailors in the Indian Ocean told of nightmare struggles with gigantic cuttlefish which wrapped their slimy arms around the ships and by their enormous strength and weight would inexorably drag the ship and its crew to the bottom of the sea unless the sailors had time to save themselves by quickly hacking off the monster's writhing arms with the hatchets and sabres they kept ready for the purpose.

Pliny went even better with his horror stories of giant cuttles in the Mediterranean, with heads as large as hogsheads and arms thirty feet long with suckers like great basins capable of holding four or five gallons apiece! These creatures were very fond of the salted fish which the sailors prepared ashore and would even venture into their camp during the night to steal these delicacies. One of these monsters, he said, was finally killed in a desperate fight with the sailors and their dogs.

Another monster which lived off the Atlantic coast of southern Spain between Portugal and Andalusia was so huge that it was believed to be unable to pass through the Straits of Gibraltar into the

Sea serpent swallowing a ship. German drawing (1598).

The once-feared cuttlefish (*Sepia*) is shown here with its typical zebra stripe markings. It can camouflage itself by varying its colour according to the background.

Mediterranean. Those who claimed to have seen it said that it had arms spreading like the branches of a great tree.

The coast of Norway was haunted for centuries by mythical sea-monsters of enormous size known as krakens. One of these was described by a Norwegian bishop as 'an animal the largest in creation, whose body rises above the surface of the water like a mountain and has arms like the masts of ships'. The Bishop of Nidros is said to have encountered one of these fabulous creatures sleeping on the surface of the sea in the sunshine. Believing it to be a large rock or small island, he raised an altar on its back and celebrated mass. The kraken remained quiet during the ceremony but as soon as the bishop had re-embarked in his ship and sailed away, the kraken plunged back into the deeps.

Reports of later date perpetuate these stories. A celebrated diver employed by the emperor Frederick II described enormous cuttlefish he had seen while diving in the Straits of Messina between Italy and Sicily. They had, he said, arms several yards long, more than sufficient to strangle a man. But he also said that they were attached to the rocks, which would put them out of the category of the free-swimming cuttle. A sea-monster estimated to be between thirty and forty-five feet long and over six feet wide was sighted by a French naval officer in the Atlantic north of the Canary Islands.

Many of these stories, allowing for the extraordinary estimates of size and dimensions recollected in retrospect from moments of excitement and fear, could well relate to sightings of and encounters with the giant squid, *Architeuthis*, largest of all the molluscs, which can exceed seventy feet in length and have tentacles forty feet long. A giant squid encountered by the French battleship *Alecton* in the Atlantic in 1860 was of this size and its weight was estimated at two tons. Another such monster, as described in an official report to the British Admiralty in 1877, was sighted by H.M. Yacht *Osborne* off Sicily.

The normal habitat of the giant squid is the deep water of the abyssal-pelagic zone of the sea. But they are also the favourite food of the sperm whale which grows up to sixty-five feet in length. Some of the males even reach eighty-five feet. Titanic life and death struggles between the sperm whale and its prey go on in these depths and the sucker scars which many whales bear around their heads and jaws

This giant squid (*Architeuthis*) was stranded at Ronheim, Norway in 1956. It was nearly thirty feet long but specimens twice this length have been captured.

are evidence of the seventy-foot squids fighting for their lives with their sixty-foot predators. Sometimes the struggle ends up on the surface and accounts for the eye-witness reports we have of great battles between whales and sea-serpents.

Once driven to the surface of the sea in its efforts to escape, the great squid, exhausted and out of its natural element, may well react agressively towards any other strange object, such as a ship or boat, which lies in its path. Its long tentacles, perhaps severed from a mutilated body, may easily be taken for the legendary sea serpents, the wide spread of sea-washed body for a piece of rock.

None of the molluscs is actively agressive towards man. The octopus, contrary to very persistent and long-held beliefs, has never been known to attack anyone. Like most creatures, however, it will react defensively when alarmed or molested or dragged unwillingly into elements unknown. The large species of tropical seas, which may have an armspread of over twelve feet, prefer deep water. When accidentally hauled up in a fisherman's net, they will thrash around, upset the boat, wind their tentacles round anything within reach seeking a grip by which they can tear themselves away and escape from such unnatural surroundings. The diver, frightening and molesting the octopus by entering uninvited into its lair among the sea caves or coral holes may find himself in the embrace of death, for if the octopus is already anchored by one or more of its suckers to rock, no human strength can prise it loose and if the diver has no means of killing it, he himself will die. The tentacles of the octopus bear suckers of astonishing power. Even a small specimen with a tentacle-spread of only a few feet can hold on to a rock so tightly as to be almost immovable without tearing it to pieces.

Like all other cephalopods, the octopus is equipped with a hard, parrot-like beak. The beak is not used as a means of defence; the octopus has other methods and it does not bite aggressively. But when driven to bite, its bite is poisonous and has been known to result

Artists' impression of men battling with a giant octopus, from *Twenty Thousand Leagues Under the Sea* by Jules Verne.

Hippo clam (*Hippopus hippopus*).

in death. So it is wise to treat all such creatures with care, for under unusual circumstances, they are capable of acting quite 'out of character'.

Another large mollusc which has earned an undeservedly evil reputation is the Giant Clam (*Tridacna gigas*), the largest of all the shelled molluscs. Some specimens may reach a length of over four feet and a weight of over 400 pounds and there are many stories of how they can trap a diver by the foot and hold him under water until he drowns. There is no question at all that Giant Clams are capable of doing this, but, has it ever actually occurred?

Anyone who has allowed a quite small clam to close its two valves together on a fingertip, knows with what astonishing strength it grips. The razor-sharp and interlocking edges of a Hippo Clam (*Hippopus hippopus*) only three or four inches in length will cut deeply into the finger before it can be pulled off. So if any diver were so foolish as to put his foot into the narrow opening between the valves of a Giant Clam, and allowed those valves to close upon it, he would be well and truly trapped. Unless he had with him a sharp knife and was able to cut into the flesh of the animal and sever the great adductor muscle which draws the valves together, he would be powerless to escape.

So we may put into the category of the most far-fetched molluscan horror stories that of the Roman author Claudius Aelianus. Writing around 200 AD, he described shellfish said to live in the Red Sea whose shells had very sharp edges or lips which closed together like the teeth of two saws and which would bite into any fisherman they caught swimming, cutting even through the bone and severing limbs at the joints. The shell he describes better resembles the Hippo Clam already mentioned which is found in the Indo-Pacific, rather than any Red Sea species, so the story may have reached him, through many garbled versions, from much further afield.

Of all the molluscs, however, the one which has been endowed with the most evil reputation of all, is not to be found among the great cephalopods nor among the giant bivalves; it is the strange and delicate sea-hare (*Aplysia*) which spends its harmless life browsing among the seaweed. These rather weird and fantastic-looking creatures which never seem to present the same outline for two moments together as they glide over the weeds or 'fly' through the water in a quivering swirl of undulating wing-like fins and frilled membranes, have given rise to many strange and sinister beliefs.

The very sight of a sea-hare was believed in ancient times to be poisonous. It could cause a pregnant woman to give birth prematurely and was therefore supposed to be able to discover a concealed pregnancy. The smell of it was held to cause sickness; to touch it could be fatal though some said that it only caused the hair to fall out from the part touched. The rich purple liquid which the animal exudes when disturbed was held to have the same depilatory effect. Fishermen in the Mediterranean believed that wounds leading to mortified limbs and even death were caused by accidentally touching these creatures.

So potent a poison were these harmless molluscs believed to contain that liquid extracted from them was used in preparing the deathly draughts with which Roman tyrants eliminated undesirable relatives, would-be rivals and over-ambitious friends. The sinister Locusta used this extract to destroy the enemies, or supposed enemies, of Nero; and later in the fatal potion ordered by the tyrant for himself but which he could not bring himself to swallow. Domitian was accused of having administered it to his brother Titus.

Even to have been known to search for or procure a sea-hare was enough to cause suspicion. When Apuleius was accused of witchcraft or using magic in persuading a rich widow to marry him, the chief evidence against him was that he had hired fishermen (at great expense no doubt) to gather sea-hares for him. He managed to convince his accusers that it was only to satisfy his scientific curiosity that he had wished to see these fearful creatures.

Of the very few molluscs which are directly harmful to man, the most dangerous are most of the cone family (*Conidae*) whose simple and elegant shells with their variety of exquisite markings make them great favourites with collectors. These molluscs are carnivorous and are equipped with a self-renewing poisoned barb or dart which they normally use to stun or stupify their prey. All of them manufacture this poison but some have a more virulent supply than others and five species are known to be capable of giving a 'sting' which can be fatal to human life.

Fortunately for man, the cones are among the very few molluscs which are not edible and therefore few people except shell collectors and those who supply them, are likely to go out hunting for them. In life, the wonderful colours of the shells and their intricate markings, are obscured by a periostracum which is often very thick. So it is only the dead and harmless empty shells, scoured and cleaned by the sea and the crabs, that people are likely to pick up on the shore.

Even so, the dangers of handling these species should not be underestimated. Of forty-eight authenticated cases of poisoning by cones investigated up to January, 1966, thirteen were fatal; thirteen nearly fatal; sixteen less severe; and for the remaining six the results are not known. The species which made the most severe or fatal stings were: the Tulip Cone (*Conus tulipa*), believed to be the most venomous; the Geography Cone (*C. geographus*); the Textile Cone (*C. textile*); (*Conus aulicus*); the Striated Cone (*C. striatus*) and the Marble Cone (*C. marmoreus*). Of these, the Geography Cone has been responsible for more human deaths than any other. Out of fifteen cases of stings by this species, eight proved fatal.

All these dangerous species inhabit the Indo-Pacific zone. The Textile Cone is common and found in shallow water, the deadly Geography Cone lives in deeper water and is therefore less accessible to the casual collector; the others are less common and *C. aulicus* is quite rare. Any live cone should be handled with great care, remembering that the poisoned barb is ejected from the canal at the anterior or front end of the animal. It is not safe to put a live cone in the trouser pocket, for at least one has been known to shoot its barb through

The Sea Hare (*Aplysia punctatus*, 6 inches long) was once a much-feared animal.

141

the cloth and into the flesh beneath.

Even the oyster, the clam and the mussel can be dangerous to man on occasion, especially during the warm months when they obtain most of their nourishment from waters rich in plankton which is toxic to humans. If eaten while their digestive tracts are filled with this substance, they can cause serious illness and even death. The adaptable mollusc can, when it must, learn to tolerate polluted water and to absorb toxic elements which can cause severe illness in less resistant humans. Many deaths have been attributed to the Edible Mussel, such as the fatalities reported from Leith in 1827 when many poor people died after eating mussels collected from the docks area. Their tolerance of copper, highly dangerous to humans, is well known and people learned to look-out for the livid green colour. In Arnold Bennett's *Old Wives' Tale*, for example, Constance warns her sister against the 'deadly green stuff' in the mussels they are having for their tea. Another tragedy at Le Havre was traced to oysters which had been cultivated in a new oyster bed located near the effluent of a public convenience. Yet when collected from uncontaminated areas both have provided wholesome and nourishing food for millions.

Of the molluscs which cause harm to man less directly, the shipworm (*Teredo*) is perhaps the best known, even though many people do not realize that it is not a worm at all but a bivalve mollusc. Its depredations have not only caused millions of pounds' worth of damage in many parts of the world, but have caused loss of life as well. Many a wooden ship which never reached its port and was never heard of again could well have foundered and sunk with all hands because its once-stout timbers had become riddled to a sponge with the tunnels of the shipworm. This happened to Drake's famous flagship the *Golden Hind* which foundered at her anchorage in the river Thames at Woolwich, fortunately without loss of life.

In Holland, before the days of concrete, much timber was used in the construction of the protective embankments and dykes which hold back the North Sea from the reclaimed land which forms a large part of the country. The prosperity and the lives of the inhabitants have been threatened again and again by the ravages of the shipworm. These little molluscs have been for centuries the destroyers of all things wooden in the sea; timber-built quays and piers, landing stages, jetties and above all the wood of ships and boats. In San Francisco Bay, to give one example of their activities, they caused damage estimated at ten million dollars in the six years between 1914 and 1920.

Copper sheathing for ships' hulls and later the increasing use of iron, steel and concrete have put a check on the ravages of this little sea-monster. But in the vast areas of the world where small boats and wooden jetties are still in use, there it will be, boring away as busily as ever.

The slugs and snails which eat up man's food in field, garden and orchard are regarded as agricultural and horticultural pests but the real killers among all the molluscs are not the giants of the sea, not the squid, the octopus or the 'killer' clam, they are the insignificant-looking little freshwater snails which carry disease and death to millions.

Of the 100 000 different species of molluscs, very few cause serious harm to man, but this small group of freshwater snails may rank among the greatest killers of the human race. Strictly speaking, they come as killers into the category of 'accessories before the fact' for although they do not kill themselves, they carry and nurture the killer which, without them, could not exist.

142

Left Horizontal view and *Above* longitudinal section of wood in which shipworms (*Teredo*) have burrowed.

Six major diseases caused by parasites in the human body are now known to be transmitted by freshwater snails. These are the snails which transmit the blood flukes or *Schistosoma* which cause the 'snail fevers' said to be man's second most common disease, after malaria.

The illnesses they bring cause a lingering death brought about by damage to the liver, the spleen, the bowel and even the spinal cord. The victims may live for years, becoming ever weaker, more debilitated and with less and less resistance to other diseases. Whatever may be the immediate cause of their death, the original and basic one is the infestation of parasites which have battened on them and drained their strength. The lives of millions of human beings are ruined by these snail-borne diseases, especially in the rice-growing countries of the world.

The strange life cycles of these parasites require a water-snail host in which to pass a vital stage in their development. They come to maturity and perpetuate their race in a human body. Their eggs leave that body with human faeces, ready to begin the cycle all over again. To survive, each one must enter both a snail and a human. Some must enter a fish as well. The fact that so many succeed is one of the tragedies of our time. Until the cycle can be effectively broken, all our efforts to conserve water, improve irrigation, bring water to new lands and improve the life of the people, are at the same time providing more opportunities and better conditions for the snails to multiply, and with them, the deadly flukes.

In Egypt, where the commonest type of fluke lives in the blood vessels of the urinary tract, the eggs leave the body with the urine, often directly into irrigation ditches and the waiting snails. It is estimated that the energy and vitality of about three quarters of the population is being drained by continual infestation.

In China, where human faeces are often used to fertilize the soil and therefore carefully conserved, vast areas are infected, but great improvements have been achieved by training farmers to expose their human manure to light and air for a few weeks until the eggs of the flukes have died. Another fluke which infects millions of Chinese

One of the intermediate hosts of the Chinese Liver Fluke is a water snail.

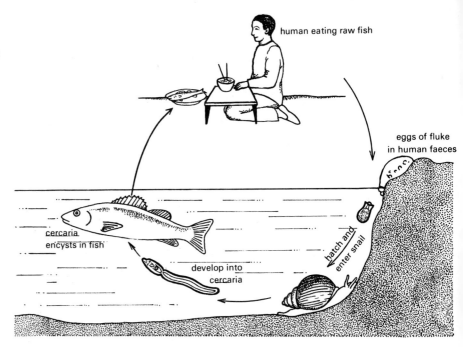

human eating raw fish

eggs of fluke in human faeces

cercaria encysts in fish

hatch and enter snail

develop into cercaria

and Japanese, almost the whole population in some areas where raw fish is freely eaten, enters the human body encysted in the flesh of the fish and is only able to complete its life cycle because the fish is eaten raw. This fluke requires two intermediate hosts – snail and fish – before it reaches its final host, man. A change in eating habits would quickly eliminate this particular form for if the fish were cooked, no danger would exist and the cycle would be broken.

Americans are affected too, especially those who live in the rural areas of Puerto Rico where about fourteen per cent of the population is infected. Some 50 000 residents of New York, mainly originating from the same area, are also sufferers. In Britain, there are occasional reports of humans becoming alarmingly ill, after contracting a similar disease, fascioliasis, which is a liver fluke infestation usually restricted to sheep and certain other animals. It usually transpires that it has been contracted by eating wild watercress from ponds and streams where infected cattle have been drinking. The eggs of the fluke, reaching the water from the animal dung, become, as they develop, attached to the stems of water plants. Even washing in salt water will not, as some people think, remove or kill the cysts.

Great efforts are now being made to find the right point at which to attempt the breaking of these various cycles. Treatment for infected humans; molluscicides to kill off the snails; exposure of human faeces to neutralize the eggs. Wherever the cycle can be broken it must be broken completely or it will start up again. And when the break is final, the little molluscs, if they survive, will cause no harm to anyone.

On the other side of the ledger are all those molluscs which, in their time, have been credited with being able to cure, or alleviate, almost every ailment the human race is heir to.

'Take five African slugs', Pliny advised the Romans 2 000 years ago. Roasted, pounded and mixed with half a drachm of acacia and some myrtle wine, they were a certain cure for dysentery. To cure a cough and also a stomach-ache, he recommended a medicine of snails – but they must be taken in *uneven numbers*. If headaches were your trouble, a poultice made from slugs with their heads cut off should be applied to the

Left A beautiful example of a cameo carved in *Cypraecassis rufa.*
Below Shell necklace.

forehead. If toothache, the small grains of sand found in the horns of snails would, if put into the hole, remove the pain instantly. A piece of octopus beaten soft and applied to a wound would stop bleeding, and fine ashes from the calcined 'bone' of the cuttlefish were effective when extracting pointed weapons which had pierced the flesh.

There can be little doubt that ancient beliefs in the magical powers of shells to promote fertility, protect the wearer and avert the 'evil eye' would have been extended to include the soft animal inside. Molluscan food has always been considered to be not only nourishing but especially strengthening and to possess aphrodisiac qualities. In both Europe and America, raw oysters have been prescribed for anaemia. Certain molluscs, particularly slugs and land snails, have been used for many centuries as remedies for an extraordinary variety of complaints.

Some of these old remedies used until very recent times in the countryside of England, still retained a quaint survival of the much more ancient belief in shell magic. To cure an ague (fever), for example, you should hang a live snail in a little bag round your neck for nine days and then throw it into the fire. You will see it shake with *your* fever which it has taken from you. Or, if you should want to get rid of warts, take a live snail and prick it once for every wart you have; then impale the snail on a thorn in the hedgerow and as it withers and dies, so will the warts.

In England, a salve made from snails was used to treat eczema, while in some parts of China similar skin diseases and the scars left by smallpox are bathed with water in which cockles have been boiled. Other Chinese remedies include the calcined and pulverized shells of river mussels, cockles and oysters in medicines prescribed for fevers, haemorrhages and thrombosis. In Malaya ground cowry shells are still used in strengthening medicinal draughts, while in India and Ceylon the Sacred Chank Shell is used by the priests to administer medicines. A powder made from the horny opercula of *Strombus* and other molluscs has also been used medicinally in the Middle East. In other parts of the Mediterranean the golden byssus threads of the Noble Pen Shell (*Pinna nobilis*) are cleaned, dipped in oil and packed into the ear to relieve earache. In Spain, a popular cure for a headache is to lay on the forehead a poultice of garden snails crushed with their shells and spread on a cloth moistened with brandy.

A seventeenth-century recipe for curing jaundice recommends a draught made from a peck of snails roasted before the fire and pounded in a mortar with a quart of earthworms, mixed with herbs and spices and infused with three gallons of ale. A spoonful of this mixture should be taken three times a day, before meals, in a glass of sack.

In 1650, a London physician prescribing a 'very sovereign remedy for the Gout' advised that his patient should 'take a good quantity of snails, prick them forth of the shells and stamp them in a mortar: then put them in a pretty quantity of salt, salet oil and sope and stamp them all well together in the mortar . . . then take same and make a plaister thereof and apply the same to the place grieved, and so let it ly for the space of three days and this will destroy the gout.'

Corns, boils and tumours were also treated with poultices made from garden snails pounded in a mortar. Even 'web in the eye' (a cataract) was believed to yield to a lotion made from the liquid distilled from snails. Those suffering from fever were advised that 'Snales which be in shells, beat together with bay salt and mallows and laid on the bottoms of your feet and on the wrists of your hands before the fit cometh, appeaseth the ague.'

146

Many of these prescriptions were country remedies used by people too poor to call a doctor and accustomed to treating themselves from a fund of ancient medical lore and superstitition, but they were not all so. An item in the London Gazette in 1739 recorded that a Mistress Joanna Stevens had been paid £5 000 by the Government (Walpole's) for the secret of her famous cure for kidney stones. It proved to be a concoction of snails, eggshells, soap, honey and herbs.

Of all the slug and snail remedies, by far the most widely used were those to relieve coughs and colds and chest ailments in general. By the superstitious, snails were believed to have magical properties, but the very long-held belief in their efficacy against pulmonary illnesses and consumption (as tuberculosis used to be called) is probably largely due to the smooth, slimy mucilage which they exude and which could be made into a thick, smoothing syrup undoubtedly comforting to dry, sore throats and bronchial chests.

At Covent Garden Market in London, large quantities of snails collected in the Lincolnshire fens used to be sold daily, mainly for concocting remedies for sick children and sufferers from tuberculosis. In the country districts people collected the small white slugs 'such as may be seen crawling on the turf of a hedge-bank after a shower of rain'. They were placed on the tongue and eaten alive. In Northumberland slugs used to be eaten alive or boiled in milk, but if taken alive they 'should be swallowed whole, not chewed, as the taste is somewhat bitter'. The glassblowers of Nottingham, until recent times, held a snail feast each year when they consumed snails to 'strengthen their lungs' for the coming winter.

Many of these recipes are preserved in letters and in household records handed down from mother to daughter, such as this domestic recipe written down in 1758: 'Two or three snails should be boiled in the barley water which Mary takes, who coughs at night; she must know nothing of it, they give no manner of taste. Six or eight, boiled in water and strained off and put in a bottle would be a good way of adding a spoonful of the same to every liquid she takes; this must be done fresh every two or three days, otherwise they grow thick.' One can imagine the nursemaid up early hunting snails before little Mary was around!

They were not all country recipes, however. In Paris in 1854, the glutinous extract of the snail, christened 'Helicin', was being extolled by members of the medical profession as a long-tried remedy for 'pulmonary phthisis'. Modern medical scientists are now studying these slimy secretions which have not only been believed in, but have undoubtedly given relief to millions of sufferers over the centuries.

The use of the purple dye extracted from molluscs as a cosmetic much favoured by Roman ladies has already been mentioned. A water distilled from snail shells and mixed with Canary wine was used in later times to 'beautify the face' and a 'face pack' for softening and whitening the skin was made from small snails dried in the sun, ground to a powder and mixed with bean meal.

Pearls, believed in as the bearers of vitality, have been used from the most ancient times in draughts to strengthen and rejuvenate, to restore health and sexual potency and to preserve youth and beauty. The pearls dissolved in wine which Cleopatra drank were taken for these reasons, as are the medicines made from ground seed pearls which are taken in Far Eastern countries to this day. Powdered pearls are made into a cosmetic paste for beautifying the complexion and rejuvenating the skin, and into toothpaste, in the hope that something of their lustrous beauty may be transferred to the user.

Right *Thatcheria mirabilis*
(1½ to 4 inches long) is
considered by many to be the
most exquisitely shaped shell
in the world.
Below Guggenheim Museum,
New York, in which the gallery
is a continuous spiral ramp,
said to have been inspired by
shell shapes.
Far right One of a pair of shell
pictures, possibly made in the
Channel Islands where a lot of
such work was carried out.

Art and Craft

Cretan vase, 1550 BC, decorated with a design of an octopus swimming amid seaweed, coral and shells, Heraklion Museum, Crete.

The textures and colours of shells, and above all their shapes, have been a constant source of inspiration to the creative genius of man. One of the oldest known sculptures of a seashell is that of a *Charonia* trumpet shell, carved in alabaster, which was found in a late Minoan burial ground near Phaistos in Crete. Its execution, though stylized, shows a keen artistic appreciation of the characteristics of the shell. In Crete also has been found the replica of a large cask shell (*Tonna*) carved in Minoan times from a lump of volcanic glass, while clay models of shell trumpets have been unearthed from many ancient sites as far apart as Knossos and Peru.

The old civilizations of Mycenae and Crete were also fascinated by the shape of a mollusc which has no shell – the octopus. A favourite decoration for the oil and wine jars carried from their factories in Phoenician ships for resale in towns of the eastern Mediterranean and Egypt was the design of an octopus whose tentacles wreathed artistically around the jar, interspersed with smaller varieties of marine life; pieces of seaweed, starfish and sea-snails. Some of the designs are remarkably lifelike; others highly stylized, the octopuses painted with huge, staring eyes, elongated heads and rows of exaggerated suckers. Such pottery was fashionable in Egypt at the time of Tutankhamen who died about 1343 BC, and similar designs are popular to this day in the native markets of Thebes on the Upper Nile. As befits an island people who worshipped the Great Mother as a sea-goddess, the Minoans used shell motifs extensively. Even their common clay drinking cups were decorated with a raised design of cockle shells.

It has been said with some truth that 'the art of the ancient world is strewn with scallop shells' and this saying could be applied to the civilizations of the New World as well as to those of the Old.

The stiff, regularly-spaced ridges and grooves of the scallop shell, emphasized by the bright light and sharp shadows of the Mediterranean scene, its symmetrical shape, the even serrations of its edge, accorded perfectly with Greek and Roman architecture. Its curves adapted ideally to the decoration of porticoes and niches. It is used in murals and mosaics, in painting and sculpture, in metalwork, glassware and pottery.

To Greeks and Romans, it was from between the half-opened valves of a scallop that Venus-Aphrodite was born, as is attested by innumerable terracotta figurines and by such larger works as the lovely terracotta Venus in the Louvre, where the goddess kneels, as if about to rise from between the wide-spread valves of the shell. A handsome black burial urn from Greece of the fourth century BC, shows her head and arms and golden hair, rising from a white scallop set upon its hinge so that the sculptured grooves fan upward and the serrations of the edge stand out sharply against the black ground.

Left Fountain at Great Witley Court, Worcestershire, in which four tritons are blowing conches to a sea-goddess holding an even larger conch. This photograph was taken in 1888, but the fountain has been damaged since the mansion was destroyed by fire in 1937.

Below The fountain at Isola Bella on Lake Maggiore near Stresa.

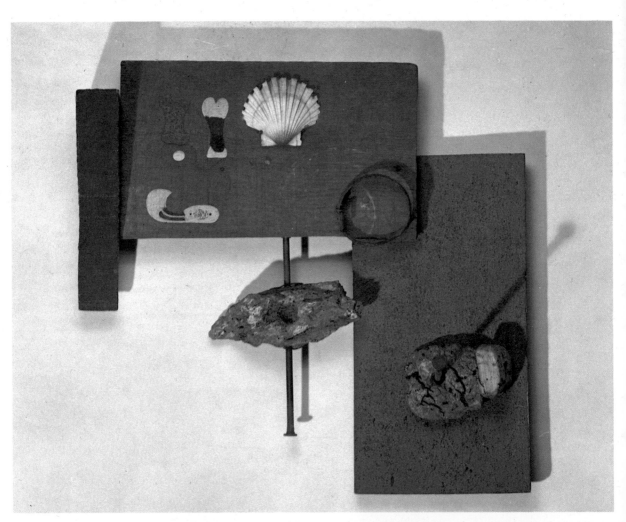

Above left Composition with a Shell by Joan Miro, 1931.
Left The Birth of Venus by Botticelli, 1485–86, Galleria degli Uffizi, Florence, includes what is perhaps the most famous of all shell paintings.

Above Pearl Fishing This painting, illustrating a multitude of shells is by Cristofano Allori, also known as Bronzino, and hangs in the Palazzo Vecchio, Florence.

Across the world, the ancient peoples of Central America made ingenious pottery flasks incorporating the replica of a complete scallop shell with the two valves closed. The lower valve formed the base and a slender neck, often with double handles for easy pouring, was set into the upper one. The Romans, too, made dainty perfume flasks of glass blown into the shape of a scallop with the serrated edges downward, set into a base, and the neck of the little bottle rising from the hinge.

From the days of Pompeii, the scallop has been a favourite device in the design of fountains. The Fontana del Api, in the Piazza Barberini, Rome, where one large shell, set upright on its hinge makes a background for the famous bee, while the other, set horizontally, holds the water it is about to drink, is one of the best-known examples. An outstanding feature of the elaborate three-tiered fountain on Isola Bella, Lake Maggiore in the Italian Alps, is the enormous scallop shells, each set in its own niche. Many of the 'stately homes' of England, too, feature shell fountains in their grounds.

The cult of St James of Compostela (see page 74) brought a new impetus to the use of the scallop device in ecclesiastical architecture. To the pagan scallops of the ancient world used to decorate tombs, coffins and ancestral altars, were added the mediaeval scallops of Christian pilgrimage. Scallops proliferated anew in the ornamentation of churches and shrines, on the sculptures of saints and pilgrims. A charming little chapel on Isla de la Toja, a tiny islet at the entrance to the great sea loch Ria de Arosa in north-west Spain, is tiled all over, walls, dome and tower, with overlapping valves of real scallop shells. The delicate tints of the shells, ranging from bluish-white and grey to pale lilac and soft rose-beige, lend an exquisite pearly shimmer to the little building.

A minor art form which subjected the scallop to some curious modifications was that of the mediaeval herald artist who designed the devices for coats-of-arms (see page 96). His work was governed by the needs which had brought about the use of these devices, primarily the need to distinguish friend from foe in battles fought in full armour. Shapes must therefore be simple, bold and easily recognizable; colours must be bright and clear. The leading characteristics of each motif used must be picked out and emphasized.

Below Close up of wall and *Below right* view of the chapel at Isla de la Toja, north-west Spain, entirely covered with valves of the Pilgrim Scallop (*Pecten jacobaeus*).

The salient features of the scallop shell are its wavy edge, its regular grooves and ridges and the two 'ears' which project from the sides of the hinge. All these characteristics were exaggerated by the herald painters. The shell was usually drawn with the hinge upward; to emphasise the ears, it was given a 'waist' between the ears and the main part of the shell, such as never existed in nature. The grooves became ever bolder and the edges more deeply undulating, until the device became a 'heraldic beast', the mere symbol of a shell. It was not until the days of body armour had passed that the scallop device began to assume a more natural form.

Scallop shell designs used in domestic architecture descended through Roman examples to Renaissance builders and were used by such great architects as the Italian Andrea Palladio and the Englishman Inigo Jones who was influenced by his style. The vogue for scallop designs over archways, doorways and windows, the shell canopies and shell niches, often added the perfect touch of ornamentation. The Queen Anne houses of England, so admired for their perfect proportions and uncluttered lines, sometimes feature a shell canopy surmounting the handsome front door at the head of a flight of broad steps. The sixteenth-century palace at Salamanca in Spain is the out-

1. Pecten.   2. Cochlea lunaris.   3. Interior of the same.   4. Mytulus.   5. Interior of the same.   6. Chama.   7. Cassis rubra.   8. Striated Lepas.   9. Cucullaris voluta.   10. Cucullaris.   11. Purpura foliata.   12. Chama.   13. Sanded Volute. 14. Purpura crispata.   15. Interior of the same.   16. Cochlea lunaris fusca.   After the classification of Requenfous.

Far left A page from *Cassells Popular Natural History*, 1870.
Left Shells painted by James Nicholls. Life-like paintings such as these enable shells to be readily identified. Top: *Cypraea pantherina*, middle left: *Cypraea camelopardalis*, middle right: *Cypraea vitellus*, below: *Cypraea tigris*.

Wall mosaic at Herculaneum of Neptune and Amphitrite, which contains a scallop shell design and is bordered by shells.

standing example of the scallop shell motif used for external decoration. The facade is lined with rows of scallop shells sculptured in stone and placed with exact regularity so that the strong sunlight creates secondary and ever-changing designs from the sharp shadows they cast on to the walls.

Indoors, the scallop motif was just as favoured. The Romans incorporated it into the design of their mosaic floors, as can be seen in the fine example uncovered in a Roman house excavated at Verulamium (St Albans). The Queen's house at Greenwich, designed by Inigo Jones in the Italian manner, has a room in which shell motifs are used to decorate the moulded cornices. Later, in the eighteenth century, the Adam brothers were using shell designs extensively in the decoration of plaster ceilings and mouldings while the scallop motif was often the outstanding feature of their famous white marble chimneypieces. In older houses shell designs based on the scallop were the chosen ornamentation of many wood carvers, whose work can be seen around the fireplaces and panelling of ancient mansions.

Furniture followed suit, especially in the eighteenth century when shell carvings on furniture had a great vogue. The graceful creations of the great cabinet-makers and designers, Chippendale, Hepplewhite and Sheraton, incorporated them, indeed, the mark of a piece in the style of Sheraton is a shell inlaid in marquetry work.

Cupboards, cabinets, escritoires and headboards appeared with scallop-shaped hoods or canopies and there were unusual occasional chairs with backs fluted and curved like the scallop, upholstered in gold velvet. The Prince Regent had a set of chairs and tables specially designed for his architectural extravaganza, the Pavilion at Brighton. They were composed of shell shapes, carved in wood and painted with designs of shells in natural colours.

158

There is something aesthetically very satisfying to the human eye and mind in the contemplation of a spiral shell. Its proportions are perfect at every stage of growth. It always looks complete, yet there seems no definite point at which it should have to stop growing. There is a sense of progression, continuity, almost of eternity expressed in its ascending coil which is comparable with no other form of growth in nature.

The spiral of a shell follows a logarithmic curve which is as nearly perfect in its regularity as is possible in an organic body. It is one of the simplest of all known curves, in which, as the spiral progresses, the diameter of the coil will grow in exact proportion to its length. It has been called the 'dynamic spiral' and finds its loveliest expression in the coil of the Pearly Nautilus (*Nautilus pompilius*) in which the diameter of each new coil is exactly three times that of the coil preceding it. To study the formation of these coils in various species it is necessary to make a lengthwise cross-section of the shells, a little off-centre so that the central column (*columella*) around which the spiral turns may be left intact.

There are many examples of the logarithmic curve in nature. It can be seen ephemerally in the curve of the wave at the moment it topples forward to break upon the beach; in the curl of a ringlet, or the darting tongue of certain insects. It is in the tightly coiled croziers of a young fern; the curve of an elephant's tusk; the coil of a ram's horn; yet nowhere so simply and clearly and in so enduring a form as in the shell of a snail.

Though asymmetrical, it is so perfectly proportioned as to deceive the eye of so great a master as Rembrandt whose etching of the handsome Marble Cone (*Conus marmoreus*) appears as a mirror image. His shell spirals anti-clockwise and so opens in the wrong direction, an occurrence which, in nature, would be so exceedingly rare as to be almost unique. That Rembrandt had failed to appreciate the asymmetry of his shell is shown by his signature on the work which he *did* etch in reverse so that it would be correct when printed.

The spiral as a flat coil, such as the coil of the nautilus, was one of the earliest designs adopted by men and can be seen in the creative work of many primitive peoples. The beauty-loving Greeks adopted it in the form of the volutes or scrolls which are the chief ornaments on the capitals of Ionic and Corinthian columns.

The ascending spiral of the snail shell has long been famed as the inspiration of the spiral staircase. It is in the broken shell of a land snail picked up from the ground or of a marine snail washed on to the shore, that man has had an ever-present opportunity of studying the phenomenon of this fundamental pattern of growth in one of its most beautiful and durable manifestations.

Leonardo da Vinci, as we know from many of his sketches, was a keen student of shapes in nature. He is said to have found, in the spiral columella of a univalve shell the inspiration for his design of a double-spiral staircase, a drawing of which is still in existence.

The columella of the West Indian Chank Shell (*Turbinella angulata*) with its three spiral folds is believed to have been the inspiration for the famous double-spiral staircase which is the chief glory of the Chateau of Blois in France. That shell shapes had been studied and admired by the architect is certain, for he also used a design of scallop shells to ornament the chimneys.

Spiral staircases permit the ascent of buildings with an economy of space unequalled by any other means except a ladder, or the modern

The inspiring shapes of shells show up strikingly well in X-ray photographs.
Top Precious Wentletrap (*Epitonium scalare*) *Middle* a tun shell *Below* a cerith.

159

A shell-covered beach in Italy.

e graceful and beautiful as well as more
nd have been in use for many centuries.
pain reached Mexico they found there an
with a spiral staircase inside. In Spain, a
en a snail staircase, *escalera de caracol*.
d, there are many examples of their use,
d compact town houses of the period.
pression is the Guggenheim Museum in
t American architect Frank Lloyd Wright
great paintings. One of the most contro-
en called just about everything, from all
to 'the miracle of Fifth Avenue'. It is
iral ramp which serves as a continuous
on the circular walls. Mr Wright paid
hell shapes and what the architect could
aid: 'In . . . shells we see the housing
the housing of a lower order of life,
what we lack: inspired form.'
edited with having given inspiration to a
mmonly known as the shipworm which
of shell material. When designing the
ping and Rotherhithe, the great engineer
known to have studied the work of the
shipworm (*Teredo*). His tunnel, started in 1825, was completed, after
many difficulties, in 1843. The tunnelling went forward with the aid
of a shield of cast-iron frames and, as the shield advanced a lining
of brick was built behind it, just as the shipworm builds its lining of
shell.

The painters' delight is to portray the colours as well as the shapes
of shells. One of the earliest examples is an Italian manuscript of the
fourteenth century which is decorated on several of its pages with
beautifully executed paintings of molluscs as well as of other animals
and plants. Many Mediterranean gastropods and bivalves have been

The Château of Blois showing
its famous spiral staircase.

used as models and there are also several species of cowries, clearly recognizable, which must have come from the Red Sea or the Indian Ocean.

The best-known shell painting of all time must surely be that of the scallop shell in Botticelli's Renaissance version of the *Birth of Venus* painted in 1478. His subject is not, in fact, the birth of the goddess but her arrival at the shore, blown by zephyrs in the valve of a scallop shell which serves her as a little boat. She stands on the hinge of the shell, about to place her foot for the first time on dry land. Botticelli also painted an *Allegory of the Shell*, in which two men carry a Spined Murex Shell (one of the purple dye shells) from which is emerging the figure of a man holding a snake. This is a curious mediaeval expression of the ancient god-in-the-shell concept (see page 63).

Two years after Botticelli painted his Venus, Verrocchio painted a Madonna (in the Cathedral of Pistoia) seated with her Child beneath a scallop shell canopy. Michelangelo himself used the scallop motif many times. Titian's *Venus Anadyomene*, painted early in the sixteenth century, is the portrait of a voluptuous nude standing thigh-deep in the sea and squeezing the water from her rich brown hair with a very human gesture. There is nothing of the ethereal being about her, nothing to indicate that she is, indeed a goddess, except the valve of a scallop shell floating nearby.

Later in the sixteenth century, the Italian Jacopo del Zucchi painted what is perhaps the first portrayal of shells *en masse*. His *Treasures of the Sea* would perhaps be better named *Figures with Shells*, for it is a beach scene swirling with nude figures and scattered with great heaps of shells, painted with more exuberance than veracity.

During the next century it was the Dutch painters who came to specialize in shells. This was because so many wealthy collectors liked to commission paintings of their curiosities and shell collections. They also liked to have all these treasures very faithfully reproduced, down to the last detail of the tables and cabinets which housed them. Sometimes they had portraits of themselves included, or of groups of admiring friends. Some of these *cabinets d'amateur* contained an extraordinary variety of rare or exotic trifles from coins and shells to sharks' teeth, polished stones, skulls, statuettes, porcelain and paintings, all jumbled up together. One such collector was Jan Govertsen who went one better and had himself painted by Cornelis in 1607 in a group entitled *Peace and the Arts*. He is depicted showing off his collection of shells to a group of figures symbolizing the Arts and Sciences, two of which are nude females. All are admiring the shells except Govertsen himself who appears to be more interested in one of the ladies!

Far more delightful are the compositions of shells, flowers, butterflies and beetles created by artists such as Balthasar van der Ast. His *Still Life with Shells* features, among others, the Marble Cone, the Tiger Cowry and the Snipe Murex, all most lovingly and faithfully delineated in a composition which includes fruits and berried twigs, a butterfly, a dragonfly, a caterpillar and a small beetle which has crawled over the edge of the picture.

Modern artists are by no means so fascinated by molluscs and their shells, though to a lesser degree many feel something of the old attraction. *The Snail*, painted by Matisse in 1953 is perhaps the best-known example, though this is really a 'problem picture', an arrangement of quadrilaterals of varying colours in which some people can immediately perceive the form, or idea, of a snail. Others do not see it at all.

Louis XVI table centrepiece made of shells, eighteenth century.

Odilon Redon's version of the *Birth of Venus*, painted in 1912, goes back to the origins of the myth and shows the goddess lying at full length along the aperture of a large conch which might be *Strombus gigas*. Joan Miró's *Composition with a Shell* (1944) features a real scallop shell in an arrangement of rocks, iron, painted shapes and colours. The surrealist painter Salvador Dali has used shells in many of his works, such as the scallop shell, from which an egg, symbol of new life, is suspended, which he places over the head of his *Madonna de Port Lligat*. Scallop shells are used lavishly in the mural he painted for the Spanish stand at the Brussels trade fair of 1970. He chose as his subject St James of Compostela and depicted the saint appearing in the heavens mounted on a white charger and leading the Spanish forces into battle against the Moors as he is said to have done at the battle of Clavijo. Among those who have made shells their subject is the Belgian artist James Ensor, whose *Les Coquillages*, painted in 1895, is a triangular grouping of large univalves including the trumpet shell *Charonia tritonis* and the Queen Conch (*Strombus gigas*) with the helmet shell *Cassis tuberosa* at the apex. More recently, the Australian artist Paul Jones has painted a number of exquisite works featuring groups of Australian and Pacific shells.

Some of the loveliest representations of shells are to be found among

Left Shell ornaments made in England in the nineteenth century.
Above A bronze sculpture, *Shell and Head* by Jean Arp, 1933, Peggy Guggenheim collection, Venice.

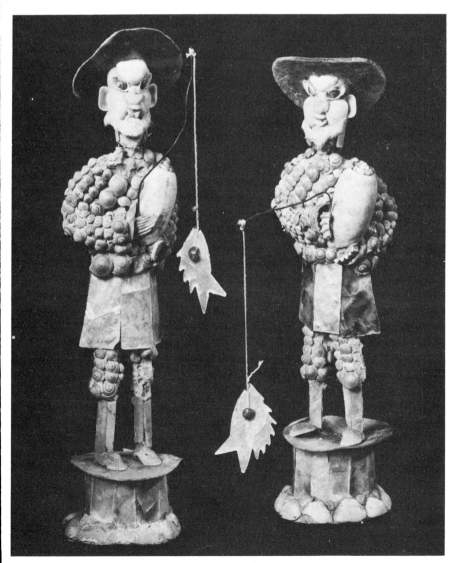

the etchings made for early books on conchology and for the catalogues of important collections. Among the work of water-colourists, that of William Henry Hunt (1790–1863) is, perhaps, unique. His paintings of 462 seashells, contained in a folio now in the British Museum (Natural History), is remarkable not only for the beauty of his artistry but for the high degree of scientific accuracy. The shells he painted with such skill and delicacy came from the collection of a Mr Barnes.

The artist-craftsmen of all ages have found some of their finest inspiration in the shapes of shells and in their unique material; porcellaneous like china or marble; translucent like clouded glass; layered like agate; pearly and iridescent like nothing else on earth. These qualities have given rise to some of the finest work of the goldsmith and silversmith, the jeweller and cameo-maker; the designers of porcelain, inlay and mosaic work; the artists of shellcraft at its best.

From Egypt, one country whose artists made little use of shell designs, comes the earliest-known gold shell jewellery, a necklace made of snail shells modelled in gold and others of stylized cowry shells, made around 4000 BC. Among the almost countless treasures of Tutankhamen's tomb (second millenium BC) is a single shell, mounted in gold.

The genius of Benvenuto Cellini found inspiration in shells for some of his most exquisite creations such as the golden chalice now in the Metropolitan Museum, New York. An enamelled turtle surmounted by a sea-dragon supports a scallop shell of gold, jewel-studded and delicately chased. On the rim, forming the handle, perches a mermaid in gold and enamel. The carving, engraving and mounting of large univalve shells such as the *Turbo* and *Nautilus* as goblets and vases has produced many fine examples, especially those of the sixteenth century made in Germany and Austria.

Artists designing for all the leading manufacturers of fine porcelain have created pieces based on shells and the close similarities in the texture of shell and porcelain. Some of their conceptions are most

164

realistic, others modify the curving shapes to stylized forms. The painters often decorated plates and dishes with delicate paintings copied from real shells, such as those painted at the Swansea factory by the well-known china-painter Thomas Baxter who had as his models the fine shell collection of the factory owner, Lewis Weston Dillwyn, a conchologist of note.

The lustrous sheen and rainbow tints of Mother-of-pearl Shell have made it a favourite material for inlay and mosaic work. The mosaic pictures in mother-of-pearl for example, made in Siam and exhibited at the Paris Exhibition of 1867, were so greatly admired that the King of Siam ordered more to be made and presented them to the Empress Eugenie. The drilling, carving and engraving of pearl shells has been a specialized craft in many countries, both east and west, producing at its best, work of the highest standard and finest artistry. Shell factories and workshops existed in prehistoric times. They have been found in places as widespread as Crete and the Gulf of California. They flourish today in the cameo workshops of Italy and the shell factories of Florida.

Cameo cutting is a craft for which certain shells are peculiarly well-suited, especially the Red Helmet Shell (*Cypraecassis rufa*). It requires a material which is formed of layers of contrasting colours so that the design may be carved in relief out of the top layer and the surrounding parts cut away to reveal a contrasting background. Certain stones, such as onyx, agate and sardonyx have this property, but none lend themselves more perfectly than the helmet shells, for the design, sculptured from the pure white of the upper layer, stands out against a background of the inner layer, semi-translucent and tinted apricot, amber, chestnut or brown. The craft is a very ancient one. Our oldest examples are both in the British Museum, a cameo cut in amethyst quartz and a simple design cut in the shell of a *Tridacna* bivalve, both dating from the sixth or seventh century BC. Cameo work flourished for many centuries, especially in Italy, where it reached its peak during the nineteenth century. Particularly fine are the pieces created by an Italian artist Ronca, who came to work in England and made cameos for Queen Victoria. Such cameos, set in fine mountings of gold, are among the most sought after antique jewellery of today.

Above Table centre incorporating fifteen shell dishes made in Zurich in 1775, Victoria and Albert Museum, London.
Below Nativity scene carved in high relief in the hinge side of an exceptionally thick Mother-of-pearl Shell (*Pinctada margaritifera*). The delicate outer edge was damaged during an air raid on London in 1941.

Rooms, pavilions and grottoes decorated with real shells were by no means unknown in ancient times. Both Greeks and Romans used shells to ornament their houses but it was not until the eighteenth and nineteenth centuries that shell decor reached its heyday with the craze for artificial caves and ruins, Palladian summerhouses, garden gazebos and romantic pavilions. Such extravagant fancies proliferated in France, Italy, Germany and especially in England where everyone who had space and the money to fill it, had to have one, often embellished with shells and costing enormous sums.

In France, one of the finest examples is a small pavilion in the park of Rambouillet near Versailles. Known as the Shell Cottage, it was built for Marie-Antoinette's beloved friend the Princesse de Lamballe. Not only are the walls and ceilings covered with elaborate designs in shells but the furniture was carved to imitate shells and corals or painted with shells in their natural colours.

In England, the Duchess of Richmond and her two daughters decorated a pavilion themselves at Goodwood Park. The work had taken them seven years when it was completed in 1739. The interior of the

Right Shell table top made
in England in this century.
Below The smallest church in
the world, the Little Chapel at
Les Vaux Belets, Guernsey, is
decorated inside and out with
shells and china.

pavilion is entirely covered with designs in shells, ranging from forma-
listic mosaics to great swags and garlands, foliage, flowers and shell
cornucopias pouring forth yet more floods of shells.

At Woburn Abbey, seat of the Dukes of Bedford, the Grotto Hall,
which was used as a dining room, is lined with shell mosaics which
took ten years to finish. The Earl of Shaftesbury had a shell grotto
(now restored) built at St Giles in Dorset. Decorated solely with
shells from the Indian Ocean, it cost him £10 000. A century later,
at *A la Ronde*, near Exmouth, two Victorian sisters were decorating
the circular gallery of their home with shell designs of birds and
flowers.

All these are open to the public and others are being restored,
but the most extravagant of them all, built for the Duke of Newcastle
in the grounds of his palace at Oatlands, near Weybridge at a cost of
£60 000, was destroyed by fire. It was a huge subterranean grotto
complete with artificial stalactites and decorated with shells. Its special
glory was a cave-chamber with a sunken pool and walls lined with
decorative arrangements of pink and white bivalve shells.

The special rooms in which wealthy collectors housed their shell
treasures were sometimes also decorated to match. Such was the one
devoted to the Elector of Saxony's collection at Dresden. It was ornamented with animals, bouquets of flowers, dishes of fruits, wreaths,
scrolls and tableaux, all executed in shells. In the centre of the room
was a model of Mount Helicon and the Hippocrene fountain, covered
with mother-of-pearl, shells and precious stones.

The most extraordinary shell grotto of all, however, is tunnelled
into the chalk of Dane Hill on the Isle of Thanet at Margate, a seaside

resort on the southernmost tip of the estuary of the river Thames.

It was discovered in 1835 under the grounds of a school, when a workman's spade fell into a hole. The hole was believed to be a disused well until it was explored and was found to lead through the domed roof of an alcove entirely covered with mosaic decorations of seashells. From the alcove, through pointed archways lined with shells, lead three passages, eight feet high and four feet wide. Two of these link to form a circle or rotunda. The third curves southward in an S bend to the arched entrance of a rectangular chamber twenty feet wide by ten feet deep with a shell-encrusted altar on the far side.

Every inch of the excavation, walls, ceilings and archways is solidly covered with millions of shells set into a cement and arranged in panels containing patterns of suns, moons, stars, double hearts, one within the other, and many symbolic designs of very ancient origin such as the Tree of Paradise, sea-serpents, the elephant, the rat and the turtle. The groundwork of the designs is filled with many thousands of little yellow periwinkles which seem to have been collected alive and set into the cement complete. They must have had a bright, golden sheen when fresh but their colour has been dulled by time and also by the fumes of the gaslights installed by the first owners when they cut a passage through to a blocked entrance in the rotunda and opened the cave temple to the public. Twenty-seven other species of shells have been used, some represented by only a single specimen. The work involved must have been prodigious, especially when one realises that it must have been carried out by torchlight.

Whatever its origin, this shell-cave, whether temple or not, is unique. It has been suggested that its origin may be Cretan or Phoenician. The great goddesses of the Mediterranean were worshipped in ancient times in shell-decorated grotto-shrines like this. No examples, so far as we know, remain – unless this is one, which would make it one of the world's wonders. The surprising thing is that this amazing work has been generally so little regarded – just one of the minor tourist attractions of a popular resort.

Shells may have less appeal to the artists and designers of today, yet it is unlikely that the shapes which have had such a universal attraction over so many thousands of years can have fallen out of favour for ever.

Shell temple at Margate.
Left Part of the serpentine passage leading to the main chamber.
Below Close up of one of the many designs in shell mosaic which entirely cover the walls.

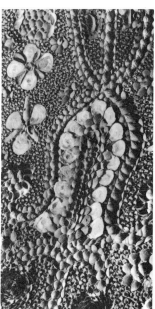

Molluscs in Language and Literature

'Semec fedde sund helm theahte ond mec ytha wrugon eorthan . . .'

Thus begins, as nearly as can be set down in roman type, an Anglo-Saxon riddle-poem written in the tenth century. It is from the Exeter Book, *Liber Exoniensis*, chief treasure of Exeter Cathedral. Although damage to the folio has obliterated the end of the riddle, there can be small doubt that its subject is an oyster. This earliest reference to a mollusc in English literature translates into modern English:

'The sea brought me forth (*or* fed me), a covering of water concealed me and waves hid me on earth (*or* on land) resting footless. Often towards the flood my mouth I opened. Now some man will devour my flesh for my skin not recking, since from my side with knife's point having ripped my hide he then eats me uncooked.'

Our language and literature are rich in references to the qualities and characteristics of molluscs. They are used so frequently in simile and metaphor, in analogy, imagery and allegory that it is not easy to read far without encountering some of them.

'Tight as a clam', 'close as an oyster', 'dumb as an oyster', 'clinging like a limpet' 'happy as a clam at high water' are similes in frequent use. 'He drew in his horns', 'retired into his shell', 'was winkled out', 'clammed up', 'cast pearls before swine', 'walked at snail-pace', 'was warmed to the cockles of his heart' or 'born to the purple'; these are some of our most familiar metaphorical phrases. We know that he has clam-shell ears and hers are shell-like. She is a pearl among women and her favourite colours are shell-pink and pearl-grey. An 'empty shell' is a figure of speech for something which has lost its vital force and meaning. When Falstaff refused to lend him money, Pistol was philosophical:

Why, then the world's mine oyster,

Which I with sword will open. (*Merry Wives of Windsor*, II. ii.)

Thus another imperishable phrase became part of common speech.

Among the many words coined from the names of molluscs are the verbs 'to pearl', to decorate with pearls or to cover with pearly nacre, and 'to scallop' which has two meanings. One is to bake food, usually shellfish, in a scallop shell; the other a term in embroidery when cloth edges are cut in a design of curved segments similar to the edge of this shell. A scallop can be a small dish; a cockle shell, a small, frail boat; the Shell, in some schools is an intermediate class (a name derived from a shell-shaped alcove in Westminster School where such a class used to be held).

We meet our first molluscs when we are very young and learn that little boys are made of 'snips and snails and puppy dog tails', that 'Mary, Mary, quite contrary' has cockle shells in her garden; and that

Mary, Mary, quite contrary,
How does your garden grow?
With silver bells and cockle
  shells
And pretty maids all in a row.
An illustration by Walter
Crane from *The Baby's Opera*,
1877.

'A noise annoys an oyster, but a noisy noise annoys an oyster more.'
We meet them later in songs, such as the ballad of Molly Malone who:

> wheeled her wheel-barrow through streets broad and narrow,
> Crying 'Cockles and mussels alive, alive, O!'

and the song of the girl on the sea-shore:

> She sells sea-shells on the sea-shore,
> She's on the sea-shore selling sea-shore shells

or in the tongue-twister:

> 'Oliver Ogilvie ogled an olive and oyster . . .'

In the days when molluscs appeared regularly on the menu, the calls
of the street-vendors were familiar:

> We daily cryes about the streets may hear,
> According to the season of the year;
> Some Welfleet oysters call, others do cry
> Fine Shelsea cockles, of white mussels buy.
>
>   (*Antient Cryes of London*)

On the themes of the snail and the oyster – the two molluscs best known
to man – poets sing, philosophers and moralists illustrate their arguments.

Shakespeare, who never lost touch with the Warwickshire countryside
of his boyhood, refers again and again to the observed behaviour of
snails. So do many poets who have roots in the country rather than
in the town. The slowness of the snail:

> The whining schoolboy with his satchel
> And shining morning face, creeping like a snail
> Unwillingly to school.   (*As You Like It*, II. vii.)

169

The Mock Turtle's song in *Alice's Adventures in Wonderland* begins with a polite exhortation to the snail to hurry:

'Will you walk a little faster?' said a whiting to a snail,
'There's a porpoise close behind me and he's treading on my tail.'

Robert Herrick likens them to the dainty feet of his mistress:

> Her pretty feet
> Like snails did creep
> A little out, and then,
> As if they started at bo-peep,
> Did soon draw in agen.

Maidens believed that they might find the initial of their lover's name formed by the track of a snail on a May morning:

> Last *May-day* fair I search'd to find a snail
> That might my secret lover's name reveal;
> Upon a gooseberry bush a snail I found,
> For always snails near sweetest fruit abound.
> I seiz'd the vermine, home I quickly sped,
> And on the hearth the milk-white embers spread.
> Slow crawl'd the snail, and if I right can spell,
> In the soft ashes mark'd a curious *L*:
> Oh, may this wondrous omen lucky prove!
> For *L* is found in *Lubberkin* and *Love*.
>
> (John Gay)

The sensitivity of the snail's horns is illustrative of both love and fear:

> Love's feeling is more soft and sensible
> Than are the tender horns of cockled snails:

says Biron, adorer of dark Rosaline, (*Love's Labour's Lost*, IV. iii.) and the eyes of Venus when she comes upon the wounded Adonis are described by Shakespeare:

> Or, as the snail, whose tender horns being hit,
> Shrinks backward in his shelly cave with pain,
> And there, all smothered up, in shade doth sit,
> Long after fearing to creep forth again.
> So, at his bloody view, her eyes are fled
> Into the deep dark cabins of her head;

One of the most tender and loving descriptions of the little creature is found in William Kean Seymour's poem 'The Snail' which begins:

> Veined and lustrous, ringed with pearl and azure,
> With amber flecked, and orange and black,
> Marvellous is the house of his abiding,
> The curved, frail mansion on his glistening back.

The protection and security afforded to the snail by its shell is another favourite theme:

> Be thou thine owne home, and in thy selfe dwell;
> Inne any where, continuance maketh hell.
> And seeing the snaile, which every where doth rome,
> Carrying his owne house still, still is at home,
> Follow (for he is easie pac'd) this snaile,
> Bee thine owne Palace, or the world's thy gaile.
>
> (John Donne)

In John Drinkwater's charming verses, there is also an underlying moral thought:

> Snail upon the wall
> Have you got at all
> Anything to tell
> About your shell?

Only this, my child—
When the wind is wild
Or when the sun is hot,
It's all I've got.

An old English rhyme has a double moral addressed to the women:

Good wives to snails should be akin,
Always to keep their homes within;
Yet unlike snails they should not pack
All they are worth upon their back.

To John Cowper, however, the shell symbolizes not security but restraint:

Ah! helpless wretch! condemned to dwell
Forever in my native shell.

In a piece of unsolicited advice to his master, the Fool asks King Lear:

'Canst tell how an oyster makes his shell?'
'No.'
'Nor I neither; but I can tell why a snail has a house.'
'Why?'
'Why, to put his head in; not to give it away to his daughters,
and leave his horns without a case.'   (*King Lear*, I. v.)

Shakespeare draws still another analogy in a saucy speech by Rosalind when she rebukes Orlando for arriving late to meet her:

'Nay, an you be so tardy, come no more in my sight; I had as
lief be wooed of a snail.'
'Of a snail?'
'Ay, of a snail; for though he comes slowly, he carries his house
on his head; a better jointure, I think, than you make a woman:
besides, he brings his destiny with him.'
'What's that?'
'Why, horns; which such as you are fain to be beholden to your
wives for: but he comes armed with his fortune, and prevents the
slander of his wife.'   (*As You Like It*, IV. i.)

When country folk saw the black slug *Arion ater* about, they expected rain:

When black snails cross your path,
Black clouds much moisture hath.

Slugs, to many people, are repulsive and slimy, evoking the ancient antipathy towards snakes and worms and all creatures which creep legless on their bellies. The Jerusalem Bible says of the wicked (Psalm 58:7–8):

'May they drain away like water running to waste,
may they wither like trodden grass, like a slug that
melts as it moves, like an abortion, denied the light of day!'

A poem 'To a Slug' by J. A. Mackereth begins:

Thou horned, lethargic, bloodless thing,
    Thou unctuous glutton among the flowers,
On dust and old death minist'ring,
    Mean comer with the shining showers,
Who dust insult the genial grace
Of Nature and Queen Flora's face,
    Yea all things buoyant, bounteous, bright;
Creep to thy dank, dark, dwelling-place
    Thou parasite of mould and night!

Other poets, however, have looked upon the poor creature with a more kindly eye:

> Now Sir Thomas the Good, Be it well understood,
> Was a man of a very contemplative mood –
>   He would pore by the hour, O'er a weed or a flower,
> Or the slugs that come crawling out after a shower.
>
> (R. H. Barham, *Ingoldsby Legends*, 'The Knight and the Lady')

To Coleridge, the slug was one of the harbingers of Spring:

> All Nature seems at work. Slugs leave their lair –
> The bees are stirring – birds are on the wing –
> And Winter slumbering in the open air,
> Wears on his smiling face a dream of Spring.
>
> (from *Work Without Hope*)

The molluscs of the sea best known to man are those which appear on the dining table, such as the oyster, which has come in for both condemnation and praise and the ones whose virtues were sung by Michael Drayton:

> The scallop cordial judg'd, the dainty whilk and limp,
> The periwincle, prawn, the cockle and the shrimp
> For wanton women's taste or for weak stomachs bought.

Oysters and a few other molluscs are the only meat we eat alive, a thought repugnant to John Gay who wrote:

> That man had sure a palate covered o'er
> With brass or steel, that on the rocky shore
> First broke the oozy oyster's pearly coat,
> And risq'd the living morsel down his throat.

In the opinion of Dean Swift:

> 'They say oysters are a cruel meat, because we eat them alive; then they are an uncharitable meat, for we leave nothing to the poor; and they are an ungodly meat, because we never say grace.'

To the gourmet, however, nothing can compare with the joys of an oyster feast:

> The pepper box, the cruet, – wait
> To give a relish to the taste;
> The mouth is watering for the bait
> Within the pearly cloisters cased.
>
> Take off the beard, – as quick as thought,
> The pointed knife divides the flesh;
> What plates are laden! Loads are brought,
> Are eaten raw, and cold, and fresh.
>
> (*Hone's Everyday Book*)

Tweedledee's song of the Walrus and the Carpenter in Lewis Carroll's *Through the Looking-Glass* is also the story of an oyster feast which only came to an end when 'they'd eaten every one'.

To Clovis, in Saki's *Chronicles of Clovis*, they are not only delicious but almost sublime:

> 'I think oysters are more beautiful than any religion . . . they not only forgive our unkindness to them, they justify it, they incite us to go on being perfectly horrid to them. Once they arrive at the supper table they seem to enter thoroughly into the spirit of the thing. There's nothing in Christianity or Buddhism that quite matches the sympathetic unselfishness of an oyster.'

James Thurber's philosopher muses, as he contemplates an oyster lying on the sand:

> 'It has no mind to be burdened by doubt . . . no fingers to work to the bone. It can never say "My feet are killing me!" It hears no evil, sees no television, speaks no folly. It has no buttons to come off, no zipper to get caught, no hair or teeth to fall out

. . . it produces a highly lustrous concretion, of great price or priceless . . . when a morbid condition obtains in its anatomy, . . . Just then a screaming gull swooped out of the sky, picked up the oyster in its claws, carried it high in the air, and let it drop on a great wet rock, shattering the shell and splattering its occupant. There was no lustrous concretion, of any price whatever, and, anyway, no oyster ever profited from its pearl.

Morals : Count your own blessings and let your neighbour count his.
Where there is no television, the people also perish.'

(from 'The Philosopher and the Oyster' in *Further Fables of our Times*)

Even the ancient belief that oysters come more easily to the dredge if they are sung to, has been recorded by several poets:

> The herring loves the merry moonlight,
> The mackerel loves the wind,
> But the oysters love the dredging song,
> For they come of a gentle kind.

(Sir Walter Scott, *The Antiquary*)

Shells have long been used for decoration in gardens and grottoes, yet in no garden can they have been used to more strange effect than those in the garden of Mr and Mrs Basket described by Sir Arthur Quiller-Couch in *The Mayor of Troy*. The entire garden was constructed from kitchen refuse, chiefly marrow bones, wine bottles and oyster shells, Mrs. Basket being 'extraordinarily partial' to oysters though not at all keen on gardening. 'The beauty of it is,' explained Mr. Basket, '. . . it harbours no slugs. It saves labour too . . .' The oyster shells are their greatest standby in garden-making because 'To be sure, you can't procure 'em all the year round, like marrow bones, for instance; but . . . from a gardening point of view that's almost a convenience. You can work on your beds whenever there's an R in the month, and then, during the summer, you can take a spell, look about, and enjoy the results.'

The limpet, easily encountered on a rocky shore, is noted for the determination with which it clings to its rock:

> And should the strongest arm endeavour
> The limpet from its rock to sever,
> 'Tis seen its loved support to clasp
> With such tenacity of grasp.
> We wonder that such strength should dwell
> In such a small and simple shell.

(Wordsworth)

In the ascending spiral Alan Dugan sees that:

> A turbine in the conch
> is whirled so fast
> that it stands still
> humming with cold light.

The nautilus, described on page 48, is not only the favourite shell of many people, but it has also inspired one of the loveliest poems ever written about a mollusc, 'The Chambered Nautilus' by Oliver Wendell Holmes. Some conchologists have condemned these verses out of hand because the poet has confused two quite different species and is scientifically incorrect. This is a very narrow view which, if applied to poetry in general would deny the poet his licence and condemn many of the finest works in the language. In his first enchanting verse, Holmes describes not the nautilus but his vision of the argonaut (see page 40) and her egg case which has no chambers:

This is the ship of pearl, which, poets feign,
Sails the unshadowed main, –
The venturous bark that flings
On the sweet summer wind its purpled wings
In gulfs enchanted, where the Siren sings,
And coral reefs lie bare,
Where the cold sea-maids rise to sun their
streaming hair.

In the third verse he describes the formation of the shell of a nautilus:

Year after year beheld the silent toil
That spread his lustrous coil;
Still, as the spiral grew,
He left the past year's dwelling for the new,
Stole with soft step its shining archway through,
Built up its idle door,
Stretched in his last-found home, and knew the old no more.

The last majestic lines voice the thought this shell inspired:

Build thee more stately mansions, O my soul,
As the swift seasons roll!
Leave thy low-vaulted past!
Let each new temple, nobler than the last,
Shut thee from heaven with a dome more vast,
Till thou at length art free,
Leaving thine outgrown shell by life's unresting sea!

Christina Rossetti must also have been thinking of these shells when she wrote:

My heart is like a rainbow shell
That paddles in a halcyon sea.

The Paper Argonaut has been most beautifully envisaged by James Montgomery in 'Pelican Island':

Light as a flake of foam upon the wind,
Keel upward from the deep emerged a shell,
Shaped like the moon ere half her horn is fill'd;
Fraught with young life, it righted as it rose,
And moved at will along the yielding water.

Paper Argonaut (*Argonauta argo* 6½ inches long), the female of which secretes a beautiful and delicate shell in which she deposits her eggs and sometimes lives.

The eight-armed octopus, equipped with grasping suckers, is symbolic to man of things soft and clinging yet smothering and suffocating, their stranglehold the 'embrace of death'. In the heyday of her colonial empire, Britain was described as 'the very octopus of nations' and the same term is applied to the great commercial consortiums and monopolies of today. When actress-playwright Dodie Smith wrote her popular comedy about family relationships, she called it *Dear Octopus*.

The strange, mysterious song of the seashell has often spoken to the imaginative mind:

And then I pressed the shell close to my ear
And listened well,
And straightway, like a bell
Came low and clear
The slow, sad murmur of far distant seas.

(James Stephens)

To Amy Lowell its song is of exotic shores:

Sea shell, sea shell,
Sing me a song O please!
A song of ships and sailor men,
And parrots and tropical trees,

174

Of islands lost in the Spanish Main
Which no man ever may find again,
Of fishes and corals under the waves,
And sea-horses stabled in great green caves.
Sea shell, sea shell,
Sing of the things you know so well.

And Patrick White, in *The Living and the Dead*, evokes in one perfect phrase, 'the frozen, frilled mouth of the speaking shell'.

What poet could fail to be inspired by the lustrous sheen of pearls? Here J. R. Lowell likens them to the stanzas of Fitzgerald's version of the *Rubáiyát* of Omar Khayyam:

These pearls of thought in Persian Gulfs were bred,
Each softly lucent as a rounded moon;
The diver Omar plucked them from their bed,
Fitzgerald strung them on an English thread.

The worldwide legend that pearls are formed from dew has appealed to many poets:

With open shells in seas, on heavenly dew,
A shining oyster lusciously doth feed;
And then the birth of that ethereal seed
Shows, when conceived, if skies look dark or blue;
Pearls then, are orient-framed, and fair in form,
If heavens in their conception do look clear;
But if they thunder or do threat a storm,
They sadly dark and cloudy do appear.
                                        (W. Drummond)

Robert Herrick has another answer:

Some ask'd how pearls did grow, and where?
Then spoke I to my girl,
To part her lips, and shew'd them there
The quarelets of pearl.

Shakespeare's Touchstone speaks with more truth when he tells the Duke in *As You Like It* (V. iv.):

'Rich honesty dwells like a miser, sir, in a poor house; as your pearl in your foul oyster.'

To others, pearls are symbols of happiness:

The hours I spent with thee, dear heart,
Are as a string of pearls to me;
I count them over, every one apart,
My rosary.   (R. C. Rogers)

. . . or of value beyond price:

The world has no such flower in any land,
And no such pearl in any gulf the sea,
As any babe on any mother's knee.
                                        (A. C. Swinburne)

. . . and to Puck, they are the dew itself, as he sings:

I must go seek some dewdrops here,
And hang a pearl in every cowslip's ear.
                        (*Midsummer Night's Dream* II. i.)

Among the lesser products of the mollusc, the purple dye is not forgotten:

Who hath not heard how Tyrian shells
Enclose the blue, the dye of dyes,
Whereof one drop worked miracles,
And coloured like Astarte's eyes,
Raw silk the merchant sells.   (Robert Browning)

'It is perhaps a more fortunate destiny', said R. L. Stevenson in his *Lay Morals*, 'to have a taste for collecting shells than to be born a millionaire. Although neither is to be despised, it is always better to learn an interest than to make a thousand pounds; for the money will soon be spent, or perhaps you may feel no joy in spending it; but the interest remains imperishable and ever new.'

In the 1830s when shell collecting was becoming the rage, a lady enthusiast wrote an epic of seventy-two sentimental stanzas eulogizing in turn various families of molluscs, each hailed by its generic name. One excerpt will suffice:

> Thou *Strombus*! hast no fine array,
> No physiognomical display,
>   To seize upon the soul;
> Sensations rise at sight of thee,
> Far other than the ecstasy,
> That beauty's winning sovereignty,
>   Inspires from pole to pole.
> (Sarah Hoare *Poems on Conchology and Botany*)

The *Strombus* which is described in her book is *Strombus aurisdianae*.

Later in the century, the Squire in George Eliot's *Middlemarch* is advising a convalescent friend: 'but you must unbend, you know. Why, you might take up some light study. Conchology now; I always think that must be a light study.'

The popularity of shell collecting inspired not only the novel-cum-textbook *Glory of the Sea* mentioned on page 45, but also a rollicking adventure story for boys and girls, *The Shell Hunters* by Dr G. Stables. It was no doubt suggested by the interest aroused in the famous shell-collecting expeditions of Hugh Cuming and takes a bunch of youngsters on a cruise of the South Seas in a brig fitted out with diving equipment and a diving bell 'as large as a lift in a big hotel'.

There have been many tales of fabulous sea-monsters in which certain molluscs have played their part; and now, even the non-aggressive snail has joined their ranks. A short story by Patricia Highsmith in *Eleven* – 'The Search for Blank Claveringi' – tells of a professor of zoology in search of a new species and fame. On a remote island he finds his new snail. It is six, eight, ten yards long when extended; its shell eighteen or twenty feet in diameter! He never gained fame by being the one to name and describe it. It pursued him into the sea and the last thing he knew was the moment when its thousands of pair of teeth crunched into his back.

Collectors and Collecting

'All collecting is a form of vice', says one of L. P. Hartley's characters; 'a substitute for vice', says another. Vice or not, the urge to collect things seems to be inherent in the human character. Hoarding is just hanging on to things which come your way. Collecting means going out and getting things – by finding, bartering, buying and sometimes even stealing. People will collect anything, from bottletops to steamrollers or concubines for the harem, limited only by the amount of money and storage space available. Some collect things for their beauty, others for their ugliness, for their value in terms of money, for prestige, to arouse the envy of their friends or just for the thrill of the chase and the desire to possess. Some collect indiscriminately, others become very selective, going for the biggest, or the smallest, or the rarest or even for the faulty or mis-shaped, for objects of some specific time, place or style.

Natural objects however, from rocks and plants to butterflies and molluscs, are collected from scientific interest and the desire to learn more about the world we live in as well as for other motives. And of all natural objects, the shells of molluscs are among the most satisfactory and interesting to collect. Not only beautiful but durable, they are among the easiest of natural objects to keep and cherish. A few highly glossy species may lose colour a little without losing their beauty – but most remain in perfect condition over hundreds, if not thousands, of years depending, of course, on the conditions in which they have been kept.

Anyone can start a shell collection right in his own back yard or on the nearest bit of open ground where common snails exist. He might have the good fortune to make a conchological discovery and find in his garden, as did the author of this book, a species of snail recorded in only one other spot in the whole of the British Isles (*Hygromia limbata*). He can make a trip to the nearest pond or stream for water snails and freshwater bivalves. He can visit the beaches of his native country for marine molluscs and he can continue his activities in any part of the world he chooses to visit. Or he can just sit at home and do the whole job by studying catalogues and buying from shell dealers or exchanging with other collectors. He can build up a fine collection at little cost – or he can spend a fortune on rarities. Whichever way he does it, he will find himself reading more and more about molluscs and their world, learning more about their ways and the fascinating stories of their lives.

All the great natural historians made their own collections on which they based their studies and many of these have formed the invaluable nucleii of the great museum collections of the present day.

The father of all the natural historians, Aristotle, must have accumulated large collections over a very wide field in order to make the

The Dutch apothecary, Seba, in whose *Thesaurus* shells were illustrated in an artistic rather than scientific fashion.

ALBERTVS SEBA, ETZELA OOSTFRISIVS
Pharmacopoeus Amstelaedamensis
ACAD: CAESAR: LEOPOLDINO CAROLINAE NAT: CVRIOS: COLLEGA XENOCRATES DICTVS,
SOCIET: REG: ANGLICANAE, et ACAD: SCIENTIAR: BONONIENSIS INSTITVTVS SODALIS.
AETATIS LXVI. ANNO CIƆIƆCCXXXI.

studies and observations on which he based his works on the natural history of animals, written in the fourth century BC. Supreme example of the Greek mind at its most inquisitive and intelligent, he laid the foundations of conchology and those of many other natural sciences. In his studies of the anatomy of animals and of their habits he was without peer in his time, for in his day, anatomy was scarcely practised and physiology virtually unknown.

Centuries later when the centre of the civilized world had moved to Rome, the writings of Pliny had very little of scientific value to add. He embellished his accounts with anecdotes and amusing stories and collected a host of travellers' tales about fabulous beasts and strange monsters which suited very well the credulous and superstitious Roman mind. He too, no doubt, had a famous collection of strange objects including molluscs, about which he would regale his friends with weird and wonderful tales. He died in Pompeii during the great eruption of Vesuvius which destroyed the town in 79 AD. During excavations, in 1800, shells were found among the ruins which may well have formed part of a natural history collection. In addition to many of the more common Mediterranean species, there were shells from the Indian Ocean and the Indo-Pacific. Even if they were not part of Pliny's collection they indicate an interest and it is known that certain Roman consuls such as Laelius and Scipio included collections of shells among the treasures and curiosities they brought back to Rome after service abroad.

The greatest collection of shells made in ancient times, in quantity if not in quality, was surely that of the mad Emperor Caligula. It must also have been the most expensive. In the year 40 AD, he led his legions to the beaches of Gaul (France) and lined them up in battle array facing the Channel and the British Isles. He had his siege engines moved into position as if preparing for an invasion of Britain. 'No one had the least notion what was in his mind,' says Suetonius, 'when he suddenly gave the order "Gather sea shells!"' He made his troops fill their helmets and tunic-laps and promised every soldier who did so a bounty of four gold pieces. These shells he referred to as 'plunder from the sea, due to the Capitol and the Palace,' and sent them off to Rome as part of the spoils of war. The rather more difficult task of invading Britain he left to his successor Claudius.

Until the Renaissance awoke men's minds anew to the glories of antiquity and the wonders of the world around them, there was little interest in the scientific study of natural objects. Mediaeval manuscripts illustrated with drawings of exotic shells suggest that in some of the monasteries, which were the sole centres of learning, there were collections of shells. An assortment of shells found in the crypt of a Mayan pyramid in Yucatan may also be the remains of an ancient collection made for priestly kings.

During the fifteenth and sixteenth centuries new worlds were being discovered, new empires were being built. Along with the gold and silver of the New World to the west, the treasures of the East were flowing into Europe. With them came a host of exotic novelties including shells from tropical waters, larger, more varied, more colourful and fantastic

Conchological drawings by Filleul taken from an eighteenth-century French plate.

than the familiar species living in the cooler waters of the temperate north. Wealthy men, dilettanti and scholars such as Erasmus, took up a new interest and began to assemble collections of 'curiosities', some of which included shells. Such collections became especially fashionable in the Netherlands where cargoes of oriental objects, both natural and manufactured, were continually being unloaded from merchant ships returning from new Dutch settlements in the East Indies.

By the following century, more and more shells were being displayed in the 'curiosity cabinets' and set out in the private 'museums' which became numerous in Italy and Germany. John Evelyn records in his diary for 1641 having bought 'some shells and Indian curiosities' from a shop in Amsterdam. He also mentions having seen shells in the cabinets of friends he visited in Italy. Some collectors were beginning to specialize and to have handsome cabinets made specifically to display their shell collections. They had no idea at that time of arranging their shells in any sort of scientific order. Their object was to make a handsome show, setting out the shells in artistic patterns designed to catch the eye and to arrange the colours in the most harmonious combinations.

By the beginning of the eighteenth century the mania for collecting curiosities was becoming so widespread that no household of any pretensions could be considered complete without its cabinet crammed with shells and other natural objects. Many of these were acquired at prices which today would be thought ridiculously extravagant. To the modern collector of antique furniture the elaborate cabinets themselves would be considered many times as valuable as their whole contents had ever been.

Kings, queens and princes, royal dukes and duchesses, the nobility and hangers-on of the courts of Europe, all had to have their cabinets and shell collections. The King of France had the largest collection, open to the public and enhanced from time to time by the addition of many gifts. The King and Queen of Sweden were both ardent collectors; so were the Empress of Austria, the King of Portugal, the Elector of Saxony, the Grand Duke of Tuscany and the Duke of Brunswick – to name but a few. Even Peter the Great of Russia acquired several cabinets complete with their collections of shells during his journeys abroad.

Important collections were also made by people of more scientific interests, many of them doctors, surgeons and apothecaries. At this period – before each branch of natural history had attracted its full-time professionals – all these studies were looked upon as hobbies or pastimes, not to be thought of in terms of a life's work. Medical men, because of their professional interests, were always to the fore in such part-time studies of plants and animals and were particularly drawn to the study of conchology.

The growing interest in conchology naturally created a demand for books on the subject, especially for books with illustrations by which the amateur collector could identify the treasures in his cabinet. Among the first was that of Fabius Columna, a Neapolitan physician who illustrated his work, published in 1616, with his own drawings and etchings. He was followed in 1681 by a Jesuit priest, Philippo Bonanni, who introduced conchology with a picture book of beautiful shells intended to delight the eye of the leisured rich. It was Martin Lister, however, one of Queen Anne's personal physicians, who was the first in the modern world to bring a truly scientific approach to the study of molluscs. His *Historia Conchyliorum* was published in parts between 1685 and 1692, fully illustrated with shells from his own collection and from those of many other well-known collectors.

So the collector at last had books with pictures of shells and could
compare these with specimens in his own cabinet. But when it came
to deciding on the correct names, his problems began anew. Classification
and nomenclature were in a state of chaos. Many names were purely
local and even nationally known ones were meaningless in another
language. There was still no universal name by which shells from the
same species of mollusc, wherever found, could be known and referred
to without risk of misunderstanding. For such a system the collector
had to await the genius of Linnaeus.

Numerous scientists had attempted to bring some kind of order and
system to the problem. The idea of using double names was being
developed. But it was the great Swedish scientist Carolus Linnaeus who,
in 1758, in the first volume of the tenth edition of his monumental
Systema Naturae, set out his simple and ingenious system of zoological
nomenclature known as the *binominal system.* In the volume he used
this system to describe and name every animal known to him, including
the molluscs.

According to his system, which could be applied to minerals, plants and
animals, each item is given two Latin names. The first is the name of
the genus (group of similar organisms) to which it belongs. The second
name is that of its species (its own immediate interbreeding kind).
Thus, the Edible Mussel, wherever it is found throughout the world,
is *Mytilus edulis : Mytilus* because it belongs to that group and *edulis*
to describe exactly which kind of *Mytilus* it is – the edible one.

In scientific works this name is followed by that of the scientist
who first described and named the species (known as its author) or
by an abbreviation of his name. Linnaeus' name is usually written
as Linné (he was ennobled as Karl von Linné) or simply designated
by its initial. So the Edible Mussel he described is known to science as
Mytilus edulis L.

The binominal system was not at first generally accepted. Old names
die hard even if only understood within a limited area. As it came to be
more widely used however, it became ever more useful to scientists in
recording and exchanging information. Though its great advantages were
realized, Linnaeus' whole system of classification and nomenclature
had its critics as well as its partisans. It has been modified, amplified
and rearranged, but basically his method of naming shells is the one
we follow today. Without such a system, the precise studies which

D.ʳ SOLANDER, F.R.S.

Top D. C. Solander (1736–82), the Swedish biologist who accompanied Cook on his first world voyage.

Above Sir Joseph Banks (1740–1820), who made many voyages and formed an extensive collection of specimens which he left to the nation on his death.

lifted conchology from an absorbing hobby to an even more absorbing career would have been impossible.

The next great stimulus to collecting shells came with the exciting mass of new material and information brought back from the first of Captain James Cook's famous voyages to the South Seas (1768–1771) during which he explored the east coast of Australia and sailed right round New Zealand. With him sailed two naturalists. One was a rich young amateur, Joseph Banks, who took with him a group of artists and topographers to make drawings of the flora and fauna and maps of each place visited. The other was the eminent Swedish naturalist Daniel Carl Solander who had been a pupil of Linnaeus. The exploration ship *Endeavour* became a floating museum filled not only with the immense amount of material collected by the scientists, but also with the lesser collections, including quantities of shells, which crammed the quarters of officers and crew members alike. Some of this material was to be kept as souvenirs and for gifts but a great deal of it was sold to the dealers who were falling over each other in their eagerness to get hold of such a treasure-trove of new 'curiosities'.

By the time the third voyage (during which Cook lost his life in an encounter with hostile natives in Hawaii) had been completed in 1779, quantities of beautiful new shells never before seen in Europe had reached the markets and the cabinets of the collectors. They were shells from Australia and New Zealand, from Tierra del Fuego, from Hawaii, Tahiti, New Guinea and the islands of Polynesia.

During the period from this time until the middle of the following century, the mania for collecting shells reached its peak. Among English collections of the late eighteenth century one of the most famous was that of the second Duchess of Portland, leader of the smart set in high society which dabbled in the arts and the sciences and took up everything in its turn with equal enthusiasm. She purchased many of the finest shells from Captain Cook's expeditions. Solander himself worked on her collection which was considered to be the finest in England and equal to the best in Europe.

It was now the regular practice for wealthy collectors to make arrangements with people going abroad in the hope of obtaining rare and exclusive additions for their cabinets. One English collector even went to the extent of having pamphlets printed giving instructions for cleaning, preserving and shipping choice specimens. Some sent their own agents abroad to search for rare seashells or the brilliantly coloured snails of Venezuela, Colombia and the Philippines which had become the 'rage' among collectors always on the look-out for something new.

Up to this time, very few collectors had been able to do their own collecting. Their shells had been acquired by purchase or exchange and very fine prices some of them had paid, not only for truly rare shells, but also for specimens now known to be quite common.

Now a new kind of collector appeared on the scene, one whose passion in life was to find shells in their natural habitat and bring them back himself – Hugh Cuming, prince of shell collectors and initiator of a new era in the story of conchology. Born in Devon, of a quite humble family, he was apprenticed to a sailmaker, but he was already far more interested in natural history and especially in conchology when, at the age of twenty-eight, he left England to set up a business in South America. After a short stay in Buenos Aires he moved to the west coast and settled at Valparaiso in Chile.

Sailmaking must have been a very profitable business there, for, by the time he was thirty-five, having spent every moment of his spare time collecting molluscs and other objects of natural history, he was in the happy position of being able to retire from his trade and spend the rest of his life doing what he had always wanted to do more than anything else: to collect. He aimed at making the greatest shell collection ever known – and he succeeded.

Having built himself a yacht which he named very appropriately *Discoverer* and taken on a master mariner to sail it, the two set out on the first of his three great collecting expeditions. The *Discoverer* was, so far as is known, the first ship ever built specially for natural history collecting, and was fitted out with facilities for both collecting and storing specimens of the plants and animals he hoped to find. He was probably the first shell collector to use a dredge for collecting molluscs and other creatures from the sea floor, a piece of equipment now looked upon as one of the first essentials of marine collecting.

His first voyage lasted eight months and he arrived back in Valparaiso with the *Discoverer*'s hold crammed with specimens, many of which were new to science. He had sailed by way of Easter Island, collecting from numerous islands through Polynesia as far afield as Pitcairn Island and Tahiti. He and his companion had gone through many dangers and had risked their lives again and again in areas so primitive that few would have dared to venture into them with only a sailing yacht manned by two strange white men. In the Tuamotu Archipelago they were attacked by natives while collecting plants ashore and had to run for their lives. They also made many friends, among them John Adams of Pitcairn, last survivor of the mutineers from the *Bounty*, and Queen Pomaré of Tahiti.

His next voyage lasted nearly two years and took him along great stretches of the west coast of South America, collecting at every likely spot, at each of which he made accurate notes and detailed descriptions. Then, with his accumulated treasure, he returned to England where leading conchologists, botanists and zoologists were thirsting to acquire some of his fabulous cargo and to describe the thousands of species new to science.

The names of many eminent conchologists are associated with the years of work devoted to classifying, describing and illustrating Cumings' collections, among them G. B. Sowerby who became a close friend, his son of the same name, L. A. Reeve, L. Pfeiffer, A. Adams and G. P. Deshayes.

Five years later, in 1836, Hugh Cuming made his last and longest expedition lasting altogether over four years. This time his destination was the Philippine Islands and the marine wonderland of the Sulu Sea, one of the richest collecting grounds in the world. In one of his letters written towards the end of his time there, he spoke of having collected about 3 400 species of plants; 3 045 species and varieties of shells; 1 200 birds and many thousands of insects, crabs and reptiles. Such an achievement by a single man had never been known before and has never been equalled.

It was on this last expedition that Cuming found, on a reef near the island of Bohol, the first two live-collected specimens of the one mollusc above all others which has captured the imagination of the man-in-the-street, the Glory-of-the-Sea (*Conus gloriamaris* see page 43).

By the 1850s and 60s shell auctions were a common occurrence and relatively high prices were paid for rare and perfect specimens. All shells were saleable. Those which did not reach saleroom standard could be sold for decorating the thousand-and-one shell-covered objects

Top Hugh Cuming (1791–1865) who formed the greatest shell collection ever known.

Above The second Duchess of Portland, who hired Solander to catalogue her huge shell collection.

A display case in the gallery of shells presented by the author to the museum at Kuching, Sarawak, Borneo.

with which Victorian England loved to embellish its homes. Still poorer specimens would do for sticking in patterns on the walls of the artificial grottoes which were such an admired feature in many a Victorian garden. The great nineteenth century auctions have never been repeated though the recent revival of interest in conchology has resulted in smaller but very successful ones being held in the United States.

After these exciting years, interest in shell collecting tended to decline. So many 'rare' shells suddenly began to become quite common as their locations were discovered and exploited. Prices dropped and shells which had been fetching £50 or £60 apiece could soon be bought for a tenth of the price. But new vistas were opening for the conchologist, new and hitherto unimagined dimensions of the sea to be explored.

Until 1860 it had been believed that no life existed in the ocean depths. Then, with the raising of a broken submarine cable from a depth of 1 000 fathoms in the Mediterranean, came the first evidence that there were living creatures in the deeps. For, to the astonishment of many zoologists, the cable was thickly crusted with living organisms; molluscs both bivalve and gastropod; worms and many other marine organisms.

One of the first of many voyages to explore scientifically the abyssal depths of the sea was that of the British Admiralty corvette *Challenger* which lasted for three and a half years between 1872 and 1876 and covered nearly 70 000 miles, dredging the sea bed at great depths all over the world. Living molluscs were collected from 2 900 fathoms and other living organisms from even greater depths. Many of these were new to science, but no 'living fossils' were found. These had to wait until the next century and the discovery of the Monoplacophora (see page 33).

Even so, the voyage of the *Challenger* was an epic in the study of marine life and transformed our knowledge of the last great unexplored areas of the world, the abyssal depths of the sea. It was the forerunner of the many surveys of the deep oceans which continue increasingly today.

Many of the great shell collections of the nineteenth-century boom were eventually donated to or acquired by museums and form the basis of the huge museum collections of today. Hugh Cuming's unique collection was purchased by the British Museum after his death. Another, the magnificent collection of Miss Jane Saul, worth a fortune and containing the finest collection of cowries in existence, was donated by her to Cambridge University. There are also valuable collections in America;

Beach and tide pools on Sanibel Beach, Florida, a popular visiting place for shell collectors.

two of the most famous are that made by Dr J. C. Jay, the first of the large private collections in the USA, and now in the American Museum of Natural History; and the renowned assembly of rare shells collected by Mrs Williams of Chicago who spent enormous sums on acquiring all the rarest shells she could buy, some of them still not to be found in any other collection. Her collection, since dispersed, is estimated to have cost her $75 000, an immense sum by nineteenth-century standards. Many more collections of inestimable value to science were made by missionaries serving in remote tropical lands.

During recent years, and especially since the end of the second World War when thousands of US servicemen returning home with shell souvenirs from the islands of the Pacific stimulated a new interest in shell-collecting, Florida has become the Mecca of the shell collector. Thousands of Americans spend their holidays there in the warm, tropical sunshine and find themselves collecting shells; thousands of overseas tourists do the same. Thousands of retired Americans spend their winters or go to live there, and find themselves taking up shell collecting as a hobby, often getting more exercise than they have been accustomed to in years. Shell collecting in the United States has indeed become a major pastime, an absorbing hobby for many and a career for the few. This growing interest has its dangers. Over-collecting of some of the more spectacular species such as the Queen Conch (*Strombus gigas*), not only by the conchologist but for food and for the shellcraft factories as well, is already causing concern. Several species are becoming

A village market in Fiji, where shells are being sold.

185

scarce in certain localities. On the other hand, enthusiasts are now being made ever more aware of the dangers and are correspondingly more considerate. Conservation of the environment is a major topic of the day and more effort is being made than ever before in man's short history to minimize the damage he does to his world. The chief complaint the shell collector has to make is exactly the same one that Charles Kingsley made in 1890 when he wrote 'the names grow, like other things; at least they get longer and longer and more jaw-breaking every year'.

Wherever there is a greater demand than the supply available, or an opportunity for cashing in on high prices, one will always find ingenious and industrious people ready to produce fakes and frauds or merely to 'improve' poor goods in order to sell them for higher prices. The world of shells and the shell collector is no exception.

Cleaning, painting, varnishing, repairing, 'beautifying' and 'improving' shells has always been a lucrative if minor aspect of shell trading. Collectors have practised these skills on their own specimens, or acquired, perhaps unknowingly, shells which have been so treated. In Holland and France during the boom years of shell collecting, some shells were so transformed that they could be passed off as new species. A common limpet shell for example, treated with hot cinders to produce a brilliant golden sheen, could be sold at a high figure as a 'new species'. Even Linnaeus was once deceived by an Arab Cowry (*Cypraea arabica*), a very common species, from which the outer layer of the shell with all its characteristic colourings and markings had been removed. The underlying layer which is of a plain violet colour had been so skilfully re-polished that it appeared like the natural gloss of a mature shell. The White Hammer Oyster (*Malleus albus*), a particularly popular species with collectors, was faked so often that many of the specimens holding pride of place in the collectors' cabinets were believed to be extremely clever imitations.

In Fiji today, such improved common cowries as deceived the great Linnaeus are sold to tourists as rare species at ten times the price of the ordinary shell. In Florida the characteristic knobby protuberances of the desirable Lion's Paw Scallop (*Lyropecten nodosus*) are carefully repaired with plaster and painted 'to restore the beauty of the shell' before selling it to the tourist.

Among primitive peoples, coveted and magical shells were often copied in less valuable materials. One of the most remarkable of Fijian industries, for example, has been the working of whales teeth into replicas of the precious Golden Cowry (*Cypraea aurantium*). In Borneo, the war coats of less affluent Dyak warriors were sometimes decorated with discs of white stone carefully ground and shaped to exact and almost undetectable copies of the discs cut from large cone shells.

In England, a fraud which was often practised by dishonest dairymen was to add the clear mucus of snails to skimmed milk to 'thicken it up' and make it look creamy. Then a touch of yellow colouring was added and the housewife could not tell it from 'full cream' milk. An even more curious fake was the manufacture of substitute snails in France, after the Second World War when real snails were in short supply. The substitute snail meat was made from waste rubber reduced to a powder, mixed to a paste, shaped to look like a mollusc and soaked in a liquid concoction guaranteed to give it just the right flavour. All that remained to do was to pop it into an empty snail shell, dress with the traditional parsley butter and serve piping hot.

The Twentieth Century Revolution

Man's exploitation of the mollusc began when those first scattered human families discovered the oyster and the mussel and has continued with increasing intensity ever since.

There had been voices crying in the wilderness but they had cried unheeded. Until about the middle of the nineteenth century, man assumed that the riches the mollusc had to offer were inexhaustible. Oysters, mussels, cockles and every other molluscan food would be there for the taking, forever. Mother-of-pearl Shell would continue to be collected to provide ever-increasing billions of buttons and novelties. More and more millions of pearl oysters would be sacrificed each year to the unending search for pearls.

After the boom years, the day of reckoning appears to have dawned quite suddenly and simultaneously in many parts of the world. Yield from oyster beds declined dramatically in Britain, France, America and every other place where oysters had become the cheap protein food of a rapidly expanding population. Everywhere that molluscs were collected in large quantities, whether for useful purposes or for ornament, alarming drops in quantity and quality began to cause concern: less and less pearl shell; less Sacred Chank shells for bangle-making; fewer and poorer pearls from each thousand slaughtered oysters; less food for man.

The rapidly-growing momentum of the Industrial Revolution was beginning to corrupt and pollute the very environment in which man lives and has his being. Toxic effluents and untreated sewage pouring direct from towns, factories and mills were destroying life in the waters of the earth. Never before in his brief history had man possessed the means to mutilate, pollute and destroy so easily, so quickly and so cheaply. Never before had he been able to upset, so thoughtlessly yet so irrevocably, the ecological framework in which he exists. The sea has always been the world's rubbish dump and sewer, but never before on so huge and unrestricted a scale.

Twentieth-century man has the means of destroying his environment at a greater rate than ever before. Fortunately for him, as well as for the mollusc, this century has seen the beginning of a revolution in man's attitude towards the world in which he lives and the other organisms which share it with him.

In 1972, the report of Britain's first Royal Commission of Enquiry into Pollution, especially in river estuaries where pollution is increasing, was published. In the same year a conference on world environmental problems held in Stockholm was followed by the first International Conference aimed at controlling the dumping of dangerous products into the seas of the world. It was held in London and attended by representatives of ninety-one nations. Fifty-seven of these, including all the major maritime countries, agreed to a complete prohibition on the dumping of such items as radioactive materials, certain pesticides which are highly dangerous to marine life, and specified chemicals, and to place some other categories of pollutant under strict control.

On a national level, lakes and rivers are being cleaned up and life in their waters is beginning to revive. More studies are being initiated into the effects of pollution in rivers and harbours and in the open sea. At the very least, and perhaps not too late, man is beginning to realize the damage he is doing.

Leading countries are investing vast sums in research into the cultivation and harvesting of molluscs. Their value is being more and more appreciated as one of the most important sources of protein food available to the ever-increasing human race.

Some countries and states have enacted legislation to protect certain species of molluscs which, along with so many other creatures, are in danger of over-exploitation. In Hawaii, pearl oysters have been under protection since 1930 and the harvesting of edible clams is controlled. In Florida, the collection of the Queen Conch (*Strombus gigas*) is controlled by law and in California permits are now required for shell collecting in the inter-tidal zone because so many beaches and rock pools have been picked clean and denuded of life. Certain Miami beaches have been closed to shell collecting altogether. In some parts of Switzerland, the Edible Snail (*Helix pomatia*) may only be collected by licence and only snails above a certain size may be taken.

Australian conservationists mounted a successful campaign to persuade the government to protect their national treasure, the Great Barrier Reef with its wealth of marine life and unique molluscan fauna, from exploitation by limestone mining. The fight against oil-drilling, now the subject of a government commission, will surely be successful too. The world is now so much more ecologically minded and the conservationists have become a force to be reckoned with. As one Australian conchologist has put it 'it is my fervent prayer, along with millions of others, that surely no body of men could be so insane as to allow drilling for oil on the greatest natural wonder left in this world today.'

The twentieth century has also seen a great revolution in the study of natural history and the attitude of educated people towards such studies. No longer could Charles Kingsley write, as he did in 1890, that 'Natural history, if not fifty, certainly a hundred years ago, was hardly worthy of men of practical common sense'. No longer could a George Eliot advise a character in one of her novels to take up some *light study* such as conchology as a not-too-arduous pastime. Nor would George Johnston, M.D., open his splendid *Introduction to Conchology*, published in 1850, with the words, 'There are not many inducements to become a Conchologist; his pursuit has always been deemed one of an inferior character . . .' But he continues by offering a crumb of comfort in assuring his readers that conchology was becoming acceptable as a respectable recreation and relaxation, 'as a resort to fall back on in those hours of idleness which will overtake the busiest of us all', and he reassures the would-be student that he will no longer be subject to the ridicule which many an earlier enthusiast had had to endure.

Such attitudes die hard, but it was those enthusiastic amateurs, persevering with their studies in the face of indifference and ridicule, who paved the way for the 'professionals' of the twentieth century, the growing body of men and women who devote their lives, not their leisure, to the study of all the natural sciences, conchology among them. Their work has revolutionized the techniques of collecting, study and research.

Conchologists using snorkels and diving equipment of every kind—from the scuba to the bathyscaphe—can study molluscs in their own habitats as never before. During recent years, deep-sea trawling and dredging have brought to light species never seen before including living specimens of Monoplacophora, that ancient class of molluscs believed to have become extinct some 450 million years ago and whose rediscovery may well rank as one of the great biological events of the century. Who knows what more remains to be discovered in the yet unexplored depths of the sea?

Museums, building on collections founded by the great amateurs of past generations, have amassed enormous quantities of shells for study. Foremost among them stands the Smithsonian Institution with the world's largest collection of more than nine million specimens. Much of the material now reaching the museums comes from the new generation of amateur collectors and field workers all over the world, more specialized and more knowledgeable than those of the past, and eager to make their contribution in however humble a form, to the advancement of scientific knowledge in their chosen field.

Shell studying is becoming an ever more widespread hobby, especially in the United States where it has come to vie in popularity with stamp collecting, and where many cities and towns, however far from the sea, have their shell clubs and members plan their holiday trips with the increase of their collections in view.

So for the mollusc, in addition to all the hazards of a polluted world and its natural enemies on sea and land, there is the human collector who, whether for food, science, commerce, or just for fun, destroys him by the billion each year.

Can the mollusc survive? Many species are being over-collected for one purpose or another. Many more are dangerously reduced in numbers due to the contamination of their environment. Despite all depredations, however, there seems little danger of any species becoming extinct even though certain over-collected ones are becoming uncommon or even rare in limited areas. The most endangered species are those freshwater molluscs whose streams and rivers are polluted by human sewage.

The mollusc is extraordinarily resilient, adaptable and therefore successful. Studies in 1862 established that mussels were able to tolerate large amounts of copper which would be highly toxic to humans. Mussels taken from Falmouth harbour were found to have absorbed so much copper from the sheathing of ships' hulls that their flesh was 'as green as verdigris'. A bead of pure copper the size of a large pinhead was extracted from a hundred of them. More recent studies following the Torrey Canyon disaster in 1967 when masses of crude oil from the damaged tanker were washed on to Cornish beaches, showed that molluscs could tolerate the oil and that some, notably the limpets, actually began to eat it. It was the chemical detergents used to disperse the oil which were devastating to marine life.

Some species of land snails, accidentally transplanted by the commercial activities of man to new habitats, have adapted, multiplied and flourished exceedingly.

Surely, the long life history of the mollusc can give hope and inspiration to man in his struggle to survive in an ever-changing world.

Bibliography

American Sea Shells R.T. Abbot, Van Nostrand Reinhold Co., 1955.
Animals without Backbones (2 vols) R. Buchsbaum, Penguin Books, 1951.
British Palaeozoic Fossils Trustees of the British Museum (Natural History), 1966.
British Snails A.E. Ellis, Oxford, The Clarendon Press, 1926.
Cambridge Natural History – Vol. III Mollusca A.H. Cooke, MacMillan & Co., 1895 onwards.
Coloured Illustrations of the Shells of Japan Vol. I T. Kira, Hoikusha, Osaka, 1959; *Vol. II*
  T. Habe, Hoikusha, Osaka, 1961.
The Commercial Products of the Sea P.L. Simmonds, Griffith & Farran, 1879.
Conchological Society of Great Britain and Ireland, Publications of
The Edible Mollusks of Great Britain and Ireland M.S. Lovell, Reeve & Co., 1867.
The Genera of Recent Mollusca H. & A. Adams, J. van Voorst, 1858.
Hawaiian Malacalogical Society, Publications of the
Indo-Pacific Mollusca Ed: R.T. Abbott, Delaware Museum of Natural History, 1959.
An Introduction to Conchology G. Johnston, J. van Voorst, 1850.
Larousse Gastronomique English Edition Paul Hamlyn, 1961.
Ministry of Agriculture, Fisheries and Food, Publications (on Molluscs) of the
Molluscs J.E. Morton, Hutchinson University Library, 1958.
The Oxford Book of Invertebrates D. Nichols, J.A.L. Cooke, Oxford University Press, 1971.
Oysters C.M. Yonge, Collins, 1960.
The Pearl King Robert Eunson, Angus & Robertson, 1956.
The Prehistory of European Society G. Childe, Penguin Books, 1958.
Rare Shells S.P. Dance, Faber and Faber, 1969.
The Sacred Chank of India J. Hornell, Madras Fisheries Bureau, 1914.
The Scallop Ed: Ian Cox, Shell Transport and Trading Co., 1957.
The Sea Shore C.M. Yonge, Collins, 1949.
Shells as Evidence of Migration of Early Culture J.W. Jackson, Longmans, Green and Co. Ltd,
  1917.
Shell Collecting S.P. Dance, Faber and Faber, 1966.
The Succession of Life through Geological Time Oakley & Muir-Wood, British Museum of Natural
  History, Dept of Palaeontology.
A Survey of Primitive Money A. Hingston-Quiggin, Methuen, 1949.
A Year at the Shore P.H. Gosse, Alexander Strahan, 1865.

Acknowledgements

Colour Heather Angel 17 bottom, 25 top; Alice Denison Barton-Barlow 24 bottom, 49 top, 56–57, 60 top, 61, 105 top, 145 top, 148 top; Author 108–9; Bruce Coleman 20 top, 25 bottom, (Jane Burton) 109 top right (Robert Schroeder); W.F. Davidson 17 top & centre; Hamlyn Group Picture Library front and back jacket, 24 top, 49 bottom, 52, 53, 64, 97, 101 bottom, 104, 112 top, 148 bottom, 156 (from Hamlyn Guide to Shells by Peter Oliver); Mallett & Son (Antiques) Limited 149; Manchester Museum (Reproduced by kind permission of Mrs. H.G. Harvey) 100, 101 top; Mansell 157; Natural History Photographic Agency 21 top, 28, 29 top, 32, (Anthony Bannister), 20 bottom, 109 bottom, 112 bottom, (Joan Clayton); Photo Aquatics 29 bottom (Hansen); Picturepoint 160; Scala 152 bottom, 153; Seaphot 60 bottom, 145 bottom (Walter Deas); Stedelijk Museum, Amsterdam 152 top.
Black and White Paul Almasy 67; American Museum of Natural History 44, 83; Heather Angel (Biofotos) 9 right, 27, 30, 33 bottom left, 37 bottom left, 38 right, 39 left, 40, 47 bottom, 58, 62, 86, 129 left, 130 top right; Ashmolean Museum Oxford 92; Author 37 top right, 151 top, 154 left & right, 165 bottom; Alice Denison Barton-Barlow 38 left, 41, 43, 46, 47 top, 48, 51, 54 right, 55, 94, 107, 111, 185; reproduced by courtesy of the trustees of the British Museum 182; Cairncross, Perth 119 right; Cambridge Museum of Archaeology & Ethnology 63; Camera Press title page, 33 top left, 35, 36, 36–37 top, 68 right, 71, 72, 88, 89, 121, 122, 134, 137, 138, 151 bottom; J. Allan Cash 76, 120 right, 185 bottom; Bruce Coleman 12 right (Jane Burton), 31, 129 right (Sdeuard C. Bisserot); Alex C. Cowper 119 left; S.P. Dance 182; Dumbarton Oaks, Washington (Robert Woods Bliss Collection) 65; Peggy Guggenheim Collection, Venice 163 right; Hamlyn Group Picture Library 9 left, 10, 11, 23, 26 left, 32 left, 33 right, 34, 39 right, 59, 91, 93, 102, 103, 120 left, 144, 155 bottom right, 158 right, 169; Mr. R. Hayes 78; Heraklion Museum, Crete 150; E. Boudot Lamotte 155 top right; Librarie Larousse 66; Mallett & Son (Antiques) 162, 163 left, 164, 166 top; Mansell Collection 124, 126, 136, 139, 181 left; Foto Marburg 155 left, 161; Dr. Paul Mellars, (Univ. of Sheffield) 15; Ministry of Agriculture Fisheries & Food 128, 130 bottom right, 131, 133 bottom; Musee de l'Homme, Paris 68 left; Museum of the American Indian (Heye Foundation) 18; National Museum, Copenhagen 73; National Museum of Wales 54 left; National Portrait Gallery, London 117, 182; Natural History Photographic Agency 12 left, 26 right, 130 left, 132, 133 top, 141, 143, 159 (L. Jackman) 90 right, 114 (J. Clayton); Hon. Mrs. Clive Pearson 182; Philadelphia Museum of Art (Louise & Walter Arensberg Collection) 90 left; Photo Aquatics 106; Picturepoint 166 bottom; Pitt Rivers Museum, Oxford 16; Radio Times Hulton Picture Library 179, 181 right; Sarawak Museum 184; Seaphot 89 right, 140, 174; Shell Grotto Margate (reproduced by kind permission of Mr. & Mrs. E. Heskett); Shell International 98; Sotheby's 95; Studios Josse-Lalance 75; Teylers Stitching, Haarlem 178; Victoria & Albert Museum 165 top.
The publishers are grateful to Yale University Press for permission to reprint an excerpt from 'The Natural Enemies of the Conch' by Alan Dugan; to William Kean Seymour for permission to reprint an excerpt from his poem 'The Snail' from *The Cats of Rome and Other Poems;* to Houghton Mifflin for permission to reprint an excerpt from 'Sea Shell' by A. Lowell; to Mrs Thurber for permission to reprint an excerpt from 'The Philosopher and the Oyster' from *Further Fables of Our Time* by James Thurber (originally printed in the *New Yorker*), copyright 1956 James Thurber. Published in the United States by Simon and Schuster and in Britain by Hamish Hamilton Limited.
The publishers would like to give their especial thanks to Peter Oliver for the loan of the shells used on the front jacket photograph and to the Victoria and Albert Museum for permission to photograph the shell artefacts on the front and back jacket.

Index

Numbers in italic indicate pages
on which illustrations occur